The Single-Minded Project

To Joanna and Amanda

The Single-Minded Project

Ensuring the Pace of Progress

MARTIN PRICE

Routledge
Taylor & Francis Group

LONDON AND NEW YORK

First published in paperback 2024

First published 2014 by Gower Publishing

Published 2016 by Routledge
4 Park Square, Milton Park, Abingdon, Oxon OX14 4RN

and by Routledge
605 Third Avenue, New York, NY 10158

Routledge is an imprint of the Taylor & Francis Group, an informa business

British Library Cataloguing in Publication Data
A catalogue record for this book is available from the British Library

Library of Congress Cataloging-in-Publication Data
Price, Martin (Business writer)
  The single-minded project: ensuring the pace of progress / by Martin Price.
    pages cm
  Includes bibliographical references and index.
  ISBN 978-1-4724-2996-4 (hbk) -- ISBN 978-1-4724-4144-7 (ebook) -- ISBN 978-1-4724-4145-4
  (epub) 1. Project management. I. Title.
  HD69.P75P672 2014
  658.4'04--dc23
                                                                    2014008256

ISBN: 978-1-4724-2996-4 (hbk)
ISBN: 978-1-03-283704-8 (pbk)
ISBN: 978-1-315-55288-0 (ebk)

DOI: 10.4324/9781315552880

Contents

PART II   CONDUCTING THE WORK

List of Figures

List of Tables

Glossary of Terms

The words and expressions used here are chosen to reflect the meaning intended in the book.

Acting in Concert: behaviour in which players working together achieve accord and 'act as one'.

Adaptation: modification of a person's or a groups' behaviour in their response to a situation.

Agile: an iterative and incremental method of project management in which the project regime responds to developing circumstances swiftly, flexibly and interactively.

Adversity: a situation or human experience presenting significant challenge and difficulty.

Alliance Working: working arrangements as agreed between collaborating parties, in which the monetary surplus is shared.

Appreciative Inquiry: inquiry that seeks the best of what could be – instead of functioning as an adversarial or adversarial inquiry.

Autonomy of Endeavour: self-sufficiency and independence in a group's pursuit of its objectives.

Behaviour: what people do and think: as individuals and as groups

Binary Leadership: two kinds of leadership are cited here: in support of a group; in support of an enterprise.

Collaboration: organisational behaviour in which parties and groups agree and practice joint action.

Collective Intention: the informed choices made within a regime's pursuit of Resolve, Dialogue and Organisation, serving to deploy a project regime's social and professional capital.

Common Cause: an alignment of project player's purposes or goals.

Communicative Rationality: the exercise of reason enabled through dialogue (as expounded by Jergen Habermas).

Community of Practice: a group sharing the goal of furthering their knowledge in their chosen field. Members learn from each other and from other sources and take the opportunity thereby to develop their understanding and offer their specialist expertise to others.

Complete Project Management: where project management achieves synergy from combining Essential Schemas (MOCS) with Vital Behaviours (HOCs).

Complexity: where the circumstances of managing a project have developed to a stage beyond complication: where complications aggregate into larger problems and difficulties.

Connected Autonomy: where arrangements are made to ensure that a project's separate elements are developed autonomously, before then being integrated.

Connection: the means by which players' knowledge, capability and progress is enabled by the dynamic linking of people, groups and other project elements. What is loosely referred to as 'Communication'.

Cultural Anchor: a source of cohesion and points of reference that are accepted; providing a community with identity and serving good order.

Dependencies: where the utility of a project management factor or outcome relies on other factors or outcomes.

Dialogue: a conversation 'without sides' in which parties 'think together'. The purpose for all participants, is to improve their understanding of an issue being shared rather than to compete over it.

Dialogue Mapping: a group facilitation process that creates a diagram or 'map', capturing and connecting participant's comment as a meeting conversation unfolds (CogNexus Institute).

Diligence: constant and earnest effort to accomplish what has been committed.

Disruption: throwing proceedings into turmoil or disorder and to interrupt progress. Can be the precursor to a course correction.

Dynamic Linking: a process for harnessing initiatives and connecting them with overall purpose and goals without there being reliance on organisational hierarchy (Denning, 2010).

Emotional Intelligence: a capacity for recognising our own feelings and those of others, for motivating ourselves and for managing emotions well, in ourselves and in our relationships (Goleman, 1998).

Emotional Maturity: a person's ability to understand and manage their emotions.

Engagement Capability: the ability of a working group to harness all their abilities and interests; to thereby act concertedly.

Enterprise: a joint undertaking characterised by risk and a boldness of effort.

Ethos: the spirit of a culture: an underlying sentiment that informs the beliefs, customs or practices of a group or community.

Facipulation: an approach to inform and influence an audience or followers.

Autonomy to perform: circumstances that provide people with the autonomy to proceed at their discretion.

Gain Chain: a chain of personal and social transactions that progressively lead to collaboration.

HOCs: Human and organisational competences that serve a project's need for adaptation through the vital behaviours of players and their organisation.

Holding Environment: a working environment that provides psychological safety to the team and encourages rational (or open) dialogue between *all* of a project's stakeholders (Culmsee and Awati, 2011).

Host Executive: an executive of an organisation into which a project regime has been embedded.

Impetus and Resolve: in assuring a project's pace of progress, reliability and success, something more profound is often needed than purpose and objectives, to sustain a project's Impetus and Resolve. An overarching purpose has sometimes to be found, lying beyond a project's formally stated objectives and is either implicitly or explicitly promoted.

Intentionality: a quality of people when focussing on the accomplishment of an objective while relying on a capability to take setbacks, to reach their goal.

Leadership: the obligation on all project players in a regime to show the way when they recognise a promising opportunity or course of action. The Nine Crucial Capabilities include 'The project's "strength"', a reference to the quality of leadership evident in a project regime.

Mid-course correction: a decision and routine required to revise or change an on-going plan.

MOCs: Methodical and Operating Competences that serve a project's need for processes and methods in managing a project.

Network of Commitments: a description of a purposeful project management organisation.

Nine Crucial Capabilities: nine vital features of effective project management behaviour.

Pace of Progress: the rate at which a project achieves the inter-related requirements for quality, swiftness and value.

Pace Perspective: the deployment of resources serving a project's priorities for quality, swiftness and value.

Pain and Gain: a contract between enterprises when acting as an alliance; in which gains and losses are shared.

Paradigm Paradox: a project organisation in which measures needed for performance improvement, despite being known and understood, are nevertheless not implemented by managers.

Process: a series of actions prescribed to achieve a defined outcome.

Project for Projects: project management as a discipline experiences frequent difficulties and failures. The Preface here ventures the idea that a 'project for projects' is needed to secure the improvements required.

Project Players: those people who share responsibility for a project achieving its goals.

Project Regime: the organisation of project players.

Projectisation: the trend for working practices in all functions to adopt project management methods.

Quality Function Deployment (QFD): a quality management schema that relates the needs of a customer with business functions and organizational processes. It aligns the leaders' to set their goals as a supplier.

Reality Distortion Field: a term coined by project engineers working for Steve Jobs at Apple. Jobs would often set unrealistic goals; many of which were then accomplished in the 'RDF'.

Regime Maturity: the capability of a project regime to maximise the pace of progress as well as sustain continuous performance improvement.

Resolute Leadership: innovative and enterprising effort to mobilise the Collective Intention of a project regime.

Resolve: the firmness of purpose and commitment to undertake a task or venture.

Restrictive Practice: the conduct of a group or interested party securing limitations to the freedom of action of another group.

Risk Awareness: player's attitudes to risk depend on many factors; ranging from the circumstances of their venture and individual perceptions, through to psychological and social influences. In their management of risk, project players need to be aware of these factors.

Schema: a procedure, system or logic used when managing a project to deploy methodology, tools or techniques.

Scope: all factors identified as applicable to a project's purpose or to the achievement of its objectives.

Self-Awareness: conscious knowledge of one's own character, feelings, motives and desires.

Serial Adaptation: conduct that is responding to a continual stream of requirements to adapt.

Serial planning: conduct that is responding to continual requirements to re-plan.

Shaping: shaping serves the need to establish and sustain a stable platform from which to initiate and develop a successful venture.

Shu-Ha-Ri: is a Japanese martial art concept and describes the stages of learning to reach mastery.

Single-Minded Project: a regime functioning as a single mind confers major advantages over a project undertaken by a group of minds. The latter is necessarily burdened with the overhead of social engagement. The term also refers to the determination, will and tenacity of project players to be successful.

Social Engagement, or Engagement: dialogue that enables a group's concerted action.

Social Interaction: the way people talk and act with one other.

Soft Skills: abilities that enable people to communicate and engage. Often seen to be a measure of a person's emotional intelligence.

Synergy: the interaction of elements that when combined produce a total effect that is greater than the sum of the individual elements.

Tacking Cycle: the sequence of actions necessary to change a project's direction or course of action.

Urgency: requiring or compelling speedy action or attention.

Value Zone: the place in an enterprise from where the greatest value to the customer is provided and from where delivery is assured (Nayar, 2010).

Venture Capital: the value of a capable project regime of able players.

Venture Shift: a project regime reaching away from a prescribed or 'traditional venture' mode towards 'high venture': to become more adaptive and agile and even 'extreme' in its irregularity and where the risks and opportunities will be greater.

Venturesome: The behaviour of player or group; driven by curiosity, enterprise, ambition and professionalism.

References

Culmsee, P. and Awati, K. (2011). *The Heretic's Guide to Best Practices: The Reality of Managing Complex Problems in Organisations*. Bloomington, IN: iUniverse.

Denning, S. (2010). *Radical Management*. San Francisco, CA: Jossey-Bass.

Goleman, D. (1998). *Working with Emotional Intelligence*. New York: Bantam Books.

Nayar, V. (2010). *Employees First, Customers Second*. Boston, MA: Harvard Business School Press.

Reviews for
The Single-Minded Project

If ever a book were written better equipped to stimulate you to 'think about your thinking' when it comes to projects, programmes and the changes they bring; I have yet to find it. Martin puts forward not only a collection of ideas that reach out and grab your attention, but also a number of subtle suggestions which sow the seeds of change in your attitude. This is one of those rare books which you will love to own and cherish more.

Paul Hodgkins, Executive Director, Paul Hodgkins Project Consultancy

Martin Price's insights into what drives a project – its pace of progress – makes a compelling case for the importance of resilience, persistence, adaptation and other behaviours whose influences over project outcomes often go unrecognized, or are ignored in focusing on more formal processes and methodology. The Single-Minded Project shows how those behaviours can be harnessed to achieve the results that organizations seek from their projects.

Ian Whittingham, ProjectManagement.com

Martin's fresh perspective to project management, a discipline still viewed as systemic and process driven, is based on an organisational paradigm of people first. Through history, projects have been used to transform difficult situations. Martin discusses why the human aspects are so important in projects and the project player's role in delivering change in adversity, introducing innovation, adapting and driving pace and performance. This is a must read.

Mark Kozak-Holland, Lessons-from-History

It is refreshing to find a book on project management devoted entirely to how people work together and the impact this has on the success (or otherwise) of the endeavour at hand. Organisation structures and politics, individual capabilities and personalities are examined in the context of project delivery to provide a thought provoking read. Recommended.

Nicola Wadham, Programme Director, FTSE 50 Company

Foreword

I met Martin Price in the late-1990s when we were both working with the same project management consultancy. We have remained friends, enjoying much animated conversation about the challenges and perils of accomplishing planned change through projects and programmes in a fast-moving and complex world. I have observed the content of this book as it has emerged since that time 15 years ago: sometimes supremely elegant and perfectly formed, and sometimes kicking and screaming (in true 'messy' project fashion). It is my privilege to write this Foreword in support of what is a great piece of work, pursued single-mindedly.

My abiding memory of meeting Martin for the first time was his assertion to me then that great project managers 'make their own arrangements'. Always one to see the obvious inadequacies of prescription-based approaches in accomplishing unique endeavours, in this book Martin has put forward a collection of ideas to guide the development of more mature and effective planned change practice in organisations.

Avoiding any sort of prescription of course is tricky if you are to communicate your ideas via the two-dimensional page – ideas need to be organised for others to engage with them.

The structure of this book I know has been its own site of struggle for Martin over the past years. Which way to cut this most eclectic of subjects (another of Martin's great sayings) in order to make the agenda for improvement clear?

I hope you find that the structure aids your understanding of what it takes to build an organisational capability for planned change through projects: the areas that crave attention, from individual people's behaviours to collective organisational behaviours.

But more, I hope you enjoy Martin's ideas and writing. I believe they will help you to think differently about what it might take to pursue progress in your world at a suitable pace, and with a collective 'single mind'. I believe in the power of this book to change attitudes and planned change practice.

Dr Ruth Murray-Webster

Preface

Project management has been credited with great achievements but too often projects get into difficulty and too often they stumble. The project management community has sought remedies for the unreliability of projects but with limited success. So we have to regard the development of project management itself as a project in difficulty. Physicians heal yourselves!

My career has been in Britain where there has been industrial decline. This cannot be explained by a shortage of resources, inventiveness, technology, infrastructure or an absence of markets and logistics. My experience points elsewhere: to obsolescent working arrangements and employment practices, the reluctance to commit to long-term investment and the shortage of determination and confidence in businesses to manufacture and sell goods and services against competition. A renewal relies on the effective management of projects.

I came to project management following a career that took me from a practising electrical engineer into personnel management and industrial relations as a director of personnel (now usually referred to as 'HR'). Later as a change management consultant I came to rely on project management; a discipline that I have continued to value. It intrigues me. It is a good example of how professional work depends on a systematic endeavour that is closely coupled with human and organisational behaviour that is capable.

Attention to both these arenas as a concerted approach, is the proposition developed in this book. In my early career in the 1980s and 1990s, the success of a project organisation was seen to be determined by how process-centric and systematic it was. Any difficulties were necessarily attributable to something, somewhere being unsystematic.

But today the hunt for competitive advantage and the adaptation that this requires is more pressing. Managing a project is always about methodology but it is distinguished by its players' innovation, dialogue, bold thinking, leadership and the adoption of new practices. It has always been about an enterprise that must question the way to proceed, respond to the unexpected, imagine routes that are un-proven and then make them effective while continuing to sustain good order. For this reason, in setting the pace of progress, processes and procedures take a back seat; with protagonists assuring success from the choices that they make and the way that they conduct the work.

My earlier professional experience has I think offered me a useful perspective on human and organisational behaviour. I recall a client once saying to me that there is only one thing more interesting than people – that is groups of them!

I know that I am not alone in seeing a project as a social endeavour. It is in this arena where the primary causes of success and failure in project management are to be found. My book labels the people who share responsibility for the success of a project as its 'players'. They engage and collaborate in a 'project regime': a temporary and often peripatetic organisation having a mixture of interests, preferences and individual contributors. For the serious project management practitioner, professional status will only be acquired when project management professionals are recognised to be sufficiently able and wholly responsible for this capricious function that they claim as their own.

A project management function is characterised by continual discovery, choices and adaptation: capabilities on which other mainstream functions now also increasingly depend. The 'change viruses' spread relentlessly. Dedicated project organisations should serve to showcase better and different ways of managing: schooling their neighbours and clients to ride their own waves of change. There is no prescription for this; however the book explores some of the principles and working arrangements needed by leaders to fully realise their ambitions.

A Vision and Agenda

At times of conflict or other predicament, an organisation's need to adapt to events will be urgent and often obligatory; its leaders being required to act promptly and urgently. But when there is no such stimulus and no immediate imperative to secure change, the challenges of decision-making are different. To achieve a long-term and sustained business and its product development, in the absence of such immediacy, an agenda has to begin with a creative vision, champions and a rationale that has been rigorously planned before then being committed as a project.

Change and adaptation are now regular features of the organisational experience: they are no longer exceptional. Just consider the energetic rise of high-impact and agile self-starter enterprises such as Samsung and Apple Inc. But also consider the closing down of businesses in Europe and the US over the last 40 years as a consequence of their unwillingness or incapacity to adapt to new trading conditions. Reflect also on the enterprise and quality management of the 'self-starter' businesses that have grown-up in the Far East. Customers and electorates alike, demand ever higher performance and reliability – placing project management as the 'value zone' of any business that is succeeding to realise its potential.

The Value Zone

This book provides an opportunity to scrutinise the Value Zone; examining the capabilities that are most crucial to an enterprise and ways to strengthen them. The potential for most project regimes to raise their performance in terms of time cost and quality, but also their capacity to adapt to issues and events, is now very considerable. Most of the large and successful businesses that thrive in the Far East are post-World War Two start-ups and remain as pioneer enterprises; operating in a society that has willingly tied its aspiration for prosperity to their employers' aspirations for global competitiveness. Their situation and its evolution has now stirred ambitions further, bringing them high performance and rapid economic growth. Europe and the US, rather than catch-up, has to re-start and harness a new resolve.

Darwin's rules apply on the global the stage. Industries, governments, civic bodies and NGOs need to anticipate and accommodate their own reinventions, adapting their capabilities through reliable project management to take them ahead of the curve. The circumstances of many organisations today have to be compelling them to respond more proactively and strategically to issues of their own resolve, agility, dialogue and organisation. Project management practitioners need to be pulling harder than they are now in this 'Project for Projects', before they can claim a place as a profession.

Perhaps there could be a causal relationship that is the result of project management being regarded by many executives as unreliable; making them reluctant to invest in innovation and change. Many of these leaders regard project management as it is conducted, to contain risks that they are unwilling to embrace. This book addresses that possibility and offers ways for organisations to become more adept, capable and confident in managing change and innovation. Its principal focus is on human and organisational conduct or behaviour. These are now belatedly recognised by the professional institutions as crucial to the success of any project.

Responding to Unexpected Events

Projects need to be conducted systematically through the deployment of methodology, tools, techniques and the use of information systems. So far as we know however, only human beings have the ability to manage, deploy and adapt these functions to suit. Project management is undertaken by project players from their own comprehension of the requirement, their engagement, collaboration, scoping, planning and execution. They have to appreciate and question the requirement in its context and conduct the work: engaging with issues while managing the pace of progress. A primary challenge lies in an organisation's response to unexpected events that may alter the project's path of progress. Such events, while always irregular, are implicit to any venture that is a project.

The Choices that Leaders Make

There can be little doubt that the behaviour of people and their organisation are the primary drivers of a project's pace of progress. Methodology, tools and techniques are vital; but as schemas they must be subordinate to human endeavour; if only because their selection, deployment and effective application depend entirely on the capabilities of the project's players. Performance ultimately rests on human knowledge, resolve, skill and collaboration. What counts most of all in securing progress are the choices that people make in deciding what is to be done, the way it is done and how the plan is revised in the light of unexpected events. It is in these arenas where we find the roots of innovation and success, difficulty and failure in the management of projects.

The success of a project strongly relies on the enterprise of those who are appointed or who otherwise choose to lead. Such behaviour is subject to the example of leadership that deploys a legacy capability at senior levels; including the sponsors and those who manage a host organisation into which a project regime is incorporated. Leaders buttress, cultivate and help to sustain other player's leadership in a regime. Their dialogue, resolve and organisational influence are crucial to the enterprise.

Behaviour of Project Players

This book relies on a distinction made between the systematic methods, tools and techniques of project management and the behaviour of the project's players; singly and when working in groups. In both, the fate a project stands or falls. *The Single-Minded Project* is devoted to the latter and examines those aspects that address the pace of progress, including: Adaptation; Alliancing; Dialogue; Courtesy and Community; Persistence; Adversity, Engagement Capability and Collaboration.

A project's pace of progress relies on the players' determination to succeed and on the choices that they make, individually and collectively to progress the work. The quality of those choices requires the players' professional ability, the dialogue that connects them, the integrity of their project management community and their capacity to collaborate.

In reading this book, I hope that you will find a new optimism for project management. A more successful future will evolve, but this will rely on the resolve, curiosity and ambition of every practitioner and their professional community.

This book is not intended as a source of learning and development material to be used in programmes to assist projects to become more single-minded, though much of it is already deployed in this way. Instead it addresses a prior and more fundamental consideration; this being to recognise where the need for learning and organisation development lie for conducting project management in today's venturesome and competitive world.

How to Use This Book

A project's pace of progress depends on an infinite number of factors. Projects are eclectic in what has to be done and the abilities needed to progress. As in an expedition, there has to be a plan, but this cannot be expected to predict what will eventuate and all that will need to be done. Planning, as General Eisenhower said, is more important than any plan. Pragmatism has to run alongside a plan; addressing both fresh constraints and opportunities as they are revealed.

All the many factors at the disposal of project players are inter-related and this, for me, makes a logical sequence of discrete topics impossible to construct. So the book is best read straight through its three sections.

Table P.1   The Nine Crucial Capabilities of a Project Management Regime

Getting and Staying in Shape	**A Project's *Collaboration*** Ensuring Joint Action – Relying On the Players' Proficient Interaction Groups sustaining a common understanding of goals and the commitment to reach them. Continual dialogue addressing requirements, scope and progress.
	A Project's *Able People* Contributing as Competent, Lucid and Committed Project Players Working with rigour and enterprise. Relying on their experience and social engagement to resolve professional, social, organisational and domain issues.
	A Project's *Strength* From Player's Leadership, Ensuring Astute Navigation and Progress With players examining issues before showing ways to progress with resolve, ingenuity, strategic thinking, professionalism, good judgment and teamwork.
Conducting the Work	**A Project's *Connections*** Enabling Players to Exploit Possibilities and Bring Synergy Building the capacity to maximise the pace of progress. Enriching the players' network, enabling engagement, scrutiny, resolve and resilience.
	The Project's *Rigour* Sustaining Good Governance, Method, Orderliness and Discipline Applying standards and techniques with practicality and agility to good effect. Relying on community maturity and open, rational and astute decision-making.
	A Project's *Pace of Progress* Maximising Both the Quality and Swiftness of Delivery Through collective intention; balancing the goals for urgency and diligence.
Assuring Success	**The Project's *Persistence*** Achieving Constancy, Despite Constraints and the Social/Political Mood Ensuring that purpose, pace and progress meet with challenges and setbacks.
	The Project's *Adaptation* Responding Effectively to Circumstances That Change Acting promptly and effectively to any call for redirection, correction or rework.
	The Project's *Maturity* Ensuring Project Reliability and Sustaining Continuous Improvement Performing tenaciously and successfully as a 'seasoned' dynamic community that sustains its capacity to improve.

1.   Getting and Staying in Shape.

2.   Conducting the Work.

3.   Assuring Success.

Each section has three chapters, making nine in all. The themes of the chapters develop the Nine Crucial Capabilities of a project regime (see Table P.1 opposite).

The reader might also choose to be more selective in their use of the book through the Glossary of Terms and the Index.

Martin Price
September 2014

Acknowledgements

This book is a product of contributions from many people: their knowledge, their insights and the dialogue that we have shared. They have all participated in a quest that began with an observation and belief that project management is always a social and personal venture, and that a better understanding of this would enable practitioners to improve the performance and reliability of all kinds of projects.

I had arrived at this view from my experiences working with PA Consulting Group as a consultant and project manager in support of businesses and private sector organisations in various programmes of organisational transformation. This and my work as a search consultant appointing professionals into senior project management roles gave me the opportunity to meet, work with and explore issues with many more experienced practitioners and opinion formers.

Throughout the period from about 1995 to 2010 – through various conversations, conferences and meetings held by professional bodies – this conviction led to the formation of a community of practice known as 'EngagementWorks'. I want to express my thanks and appreciation to all who played a part in that rich and extended experience in which we exchanged and developed ideas about the human and organisational behaviour to be found in project organisations and their significance. They included John Algar, Sukhwant Bal, Lisa Talifero, Gordon Mackellar, Stephen Bradley, Penny Pullen, John Slater, Tim Mortimer, Brenda Hales, Jane Parslow, Ruth Murray-Webster, Tim O'Connor and Peter Kenaghan.

At this time, also as a director of the Project Management Institute (PMI) UK Chapter, I came to know many practitioners through the monthly meetings that I convened over a period of six years in London. Those speakers, and the discussions with Chapter members that followed, provided an abundance of inspiration, new ideas and opportunities to engage with many stories of members' experiences as practitioners.

Over this time I met and sometimes worked with many other able people, these included John Greenwood, Nicola Wadham, Chris Field, Adrian Dooley,

Peter Simon, David Hillson, Franco Gaurrella, Kevin Philips, Mark Winter, Ranjit Sidhu, Anna Snelling, Arnold McCutcheon, Mark Kozak-Holland, Bob Buttrick, Kevin Potts, Geoff Reiss, Adrian Tillin, Donnie McNicol, Christopher Worsley, Terry Williams, Peter Morris, Andy Mais, Trevor Band, Sheilina Somani, Chris Cattaway, Dave Congleton, Bob Owen, David Partington, Kailash Awati, Piotr Plewinski, Malgorzata Kusyk, Mark Crowne, Nick Fewings, Rodney Turner and Peter Taylor. To them and many others I also extend my sincere thanks; acknowledging their contribution to the ideas, stories, principles, strategies and working practices recounted and developed here.

In devising and writing this book, I have been fortunate to have the help of a number of able practitioners, authors and good friends. As a first-time author, I am particularly indebted to John Algar, John Greenwood, Pete Harpum, Mark Kozak-Holland, Gordon Mackellar, Ruth Murray-Webster, Tim O'Connor, Ian Whittingham, Nigel Wright and Jonathan Norman, Gower's commissioning editor for this text, who has been a tower of strength for my work as a cub writer.

My wife, Sarah, has provided me with insightful help and advice: particularly as a critic of my writing. She has endured much and offered, as an outsider to project management, a liveliness and greater clarity to the narrative. Without her, the book would simply not exist.

Introduction

As someone once wrote at an earlier time in history, 'It was the best of times, it was the worst of times, it was the age of wisdom, it was the age of foolishness' (Dickens, 2003). Today, for the capable and professional project manager, it is the best of times, with the demand for able project management professionals now stronger than ever. But it is also true that many of their customers and users are dissatisfied and even disillusioned by experiences of a project's difficulties and failure.

This makes it also the worst of times, with this predicament apparently endemic to a large part of the project management community. As Sir Peter Gershon (founder of the Office for Government Commerce and now chairman of Tate & Lyle) said at the 2010 Association for Project Management (APM) National Conference: 'Projects continue to fail for the same boring, repetitive reasons' (Wilkinshaw, 2011).

Projects, large and small, grow in importance serving our commercial enterprise, public and civic developments. Projects are crucial for the generation of wealth, infrastructure and other benefits and on which we rely for delivering the fruits of the world's enterprise and public investment. These pressing demands for innovation, economy, reliability, wealth creation and the conservation of global resources, have in recent years radically altered the landscape of project management. But the recurrence of project difficulties and failures are now regarded by many project sponsors and customers as unacceptable; and this despite massive investment in project management research, training, tools and techniques. Markets that require and eventually pay for project management are emphatic in calling for significant improvements to project management capability and their pace of progress.

Professor Terry Williams, Dean at Hull University Business School, and others in recent research into culture and project management found that:

> *the majority of project activities and resource allocation involved in these projects is being channelled towards technical aspects of the project that are wrongly perceived to be more critical to the success of*

the project than social factors. This common misconception serves as one of the reasons why this research exercise emphasises the need for a focus on a greater appreciation on the social and political context of project implementation. (Williams in Ojiako et al., 2012: 10)

Peter Morris, Professor of Construction at University College, London, claims that 'Projects ultimately are managed by people. Not systems, not contracts – people. People working in organisations, doing jobs, operating systems, preparing plans, making decisions, communicating' (Morris, 1994: 303).

Project players – all those who share responsibility for a project's results; frequently find themselves in places and circumstances that could not have been anticipated. Such situations call for thoughtful, skilful, spirited dialogue and critical choices; to build on what must always be a limited comprehension of the issues. Project players must be able to cope with uncertainties, ambiguity, controversy. They need also to be able to count on the discernment of colleagues in a mature, professional organisation and strong community.

Pace and Reliability

This book addresses the capacity of a project management organisation to manage the pace of a project's progress – an aspect of project management not explicitly provided for in recognised professional standards. A project's pace of progress (see Chapter 6) can be maximised from the 'Pace Perspective' described later in this book. It addresses the choices made by a project regime in seeking to satisfy the sense of urgency and need for diligence in achieving its goals. The Pace Perspective can be used to drive performance, informed by and informing every decision made in managing a project.

A project can be usefully compared to a mountaineering expedition. Both rely on funding, planning, equipment and well-prepared and trained participants. However, it is the social engagement, collaboration and decision-making: the behaviour of the climbers and other members of the expedition individually and as groups, that will be the primary determinants of both success and failure. They lie in the will and potential for dialogue, resolve and the organisation of the venture. As in an expedition, a project must make its way through virgin territory, where the routes to progress must first be discovered.

Project professionals are needed as specialists and also for their participation and leadership as members of a community of players. This book shows that community behaviour and team play are as important as the contributions of individuals from their thinking, propositions and leadership.

Players' Behaviour and Collective Responses

During project execution, contingency and other emergent matters can turn out to be the most critical issues; bringing challenge and often controversy to what is to be done and how. The reliance on competence, conversation and candour is high; every situation being unique and dependent on the quality of thinking and working relationships. It is the players', their thinking and deciding together, who must take responsibility for their conduct and fate of their project.

In addressing emergent and unexpected situations, project management standards and processes have little to offer. Under these circumstances, recognised methodologies cannot alone be expected to sustain progress. The values and routines of a workplace culture will sometimes manoeuvre much of the players' behaviour, to good effect or not. It will be the quality of the players' resolve, thinking, dialogue and organisation, exercised by player's leadership that will determine the outcome.

Skilful and professional care can inject strong pace into the work; reducing downside risks and avoiding unnecessary and wasteful political manoeuvring. This book offers route maps to bring progress that is strongly paced and reliable.

Initiatives to raise the capability of a project management enterprise are prompted by the sponsor, the competence of individuals and the capability of their organisation. In the Occident, principally in North America and Europe, there is a tradition to start by giving attention to competence; in the Orient concern for organisational capability and results tends to be the first consideration – this then stimulating attention to the personal and professional development of players.

While the recognised competences of project players are important, as detailed in the *APM Competence Framework* (APM, 2008) and PMI *Project Management Competence Development Framework* (Yinger, 2007), much more is required for an organisation to thrive. Project management depends upon venturesome patterns of behaviour by people and organisations stimulating curiosity, enquiry, scepticism, tenacity, bravery, compromise, adaptation, engagement and collaboration. These vital behaviours provide the life-blood of any project organisation. They bring the necessary purpose, energy, imagination and resolution necessary to exploit recognised standards, knowledge and competences.

A Common Methodology: Not Enough

Many leading practitioners have been examining afresh the net value to a project regime of adopting a universal project management methodology. While seeking to reap the benefits of compliance with universally applicable standards, they must also reckon with the dangers of such a policy threatening project player's freedom of action. The dilemma for them is that while not wishing to loosen the rigour of a common methodology, they also recognise the value of the players themselves as resolute professionals using their own discretion as professionals in their managing.

A project management office (PMO), if simply acting as custodian of tools and standards, is unlikely to call on players to comply while at the same time 'waiving through' practices that are non-compliant. So what is to be done? The issue addressed here arises from the all-too-common and dangerous assumption that project management is a methodology only.

There is very much more to project management than this. Methodology, rather than a dominant factor, needs to be regarded as one of a number of features; all of which can bring strengths or weaknesses; depending on how well they are chosen and applied. Other features of project management include the players' resolve, dialogue and organisation.

A project professional or a PMO, in judging the efficacy of a project management endeavour, must take account of all that is required to progress a project. If we are to judge the proficiency of a project regime simply by its deployment of methodology and its compliance with standards, a distorted picture will emerge of an endeavour that is little more than a customised procedure. Such an interpretation is of course absurd in its failure to recognise the adaptation, ingenuity and re-planning that are always required. A project is subject to irregularity that demands experienced observation and decision-making; placing the players' capacity for social engagement, conversation and collaboration centre stage.

Root Causes of Triumph and Failure

All aspects of project management somehow need to aggregate in our minds into a greater whole; something that the project management institutions have yet to devise. In a formative period of the modern epoch of project management, in the 1960s, 1970s and 1980s, there was a preoccupation with new techniques to facilitate such matters as planning, control, earned value, integrated logistics, systems analysis and value management. More recently the use of information technology (IT) has been at the forefront of new thinking. However, when project professionals discuss their experiences working in a project regime, the issues of resolve, ability, collaboration, organisation, repeated mistakes, imagination, teamwork and communication, more often dominate the conversation.

These are not novel issues recently added to human endeavour. Any student of history will confirm that from before the Trojan Wars they have been amongst the root causes of both triumph and failure; and they remain so. For the project management community, such issues arising from people's and groups' behaviour have to be the primary focus of our attention in an increasingly competitive, pressured and ambiguous working environment.

A project regime needs to respond to events and emergent issues judiciously and without undue delay. It needs to act as one and in concert: to be single-minded. The idea of *The Single-Minded Project* is one that is able to work collectively and resolutely in this way. This book offers some fresh insights and images describing the behaviours required. As the book unfolds, readers will be able to appreciate, perhaps more fully than before, why and how an organisation's single-mindedness is so important as well as what can be done to make it so.

This is not an academic work: it is the product of the experience of many practitioners. Nevertheless, it does rely on the value that comes from academic contributors to whom many references are made. The focus of attention is the execution phase of a project, although many of the principles described are applicable elsewhere in the life-cycle and to the functioning of programme management.

A paradigm shift is now required in our understanding of this discipline that recognises that a project regime needs to deploy the whole anatomy of its discipline. Methods, tools and other schemas are important, but they are far from sufficient. Only through the integration of both schemas and to human and organisational behaviour, can practitioners expect to realise a project's potential for reliably and success.

Terms Used in this Book

PROJECT PLAYER

Stakeholders are those parties who have an interest or 'stake' in a project enterprise or represent those who have such an interest. They participate in the management of a project *or* have a material interest in its success *or* occupy both of these roles. When actively participating and sharing in the management and leadership of a project their role is as a 'project player'. As such they are participating and sharing responsibility for its management and leadership. Their role can be temporary but never part-time. They may sometimes nominate a proxy. Project players are drawn from:

- members of a project manager's core group;

- stakeholders or representatives of stakeholders;

- representing contributing functions – e.g. finance, IT, engineering, human resource management (HRM), design, marketing;

- customers or users;

- suppliers;

- regulators.

Project players act and interact as primary contributors to the conduct, decision-making, pace and organisation of the project. A stakeholder transacting particular contracts or commitments may also take the part of project player – thereby sharing wider responsibilities for a project's overall success. Players need to be recognised as such and be aware of the identities of all other players.

PROJECT REGIME

The reference here is to a project's organisation of project players (see above) who together carry responsibility under the authority of a project manager for comprehending and assessing the project's context or environment, shaping the project, determining working arrangements, resolving key issues, solving problems, accommodating interests, execution and delivering on promises. The role of the project manager is to ensure that project players are sufficiently experienced to share responsibility for managing the work, by engaging together, collaborating, driving and contributing to decisions. The project manager may choose to appoint a core group of project players to be responsible for central functions. Membership typically changes during the life-cycle and in response to the issues being addressed (see '"The Project Team": An Abiding Myth' in Chapter 2).

Professional Pointers

- Project management maturity is its capacity to maximise its pace of progress.

- Focus on a greater appreciation of the social and political context of project implementation.

- 'Projects ultimately are managed by people. Not systems, not contracts – people'.

- Projects frequently find themselves in circumstances that could not have been anticipated.

- A paradigm shift is now required in our understanding of this discipline.

- As in an expedition, a project must make its way through virgin territory where the routes to progress must first be discovered.

- There is an all-too-common asssumption that project management is merely a methodology.

- Why and how an organisation's single-mindedness is so important.

- A paradigm shift is now required in our understanding of this discipline.

- A project regime needs to deploy the whole anatomy of its discipline.

References

APM. (2008). *APM Competence Framework.* High Wycombe: Association for Project Management.

Dickens, C. (2003). *A Tale of Two Cities.* London: CRW Publishing.

Morris, P.W.G. (1994). *The Management of Projects.* London: Thomas Telford.

Ojiako, U., Chipulu, M., Gardiner, P., Williams, T., Anantatmula, V., Mota, C., Maguire, S., Shou, Y., Nwilo, P. and Peansupap, V. (2012). *Cultural Imperatives in Perceptions of Project Success and Failure.* Newtown Square, PA: Project Management Institute.

Wilkinshaw, S. (2011). Envisaging a world where all projects are boring. Retrieved 20 December 2012 from The Blog: http://www.apm.org.uk/blog.

Yinger, C.C. (2007). *Project Management Competence Development Framework.* Newtown Square, PA: Project Management Institute.

PART I
Getting and Staying in Shape

Chapter 1
A Project's Collaboration

Ensuring Joint Action – Relying On the Players'
Proficient Interaction

Groups sustaining a common understanding of goals and the commitment to reach them. Continual dialogue addressing requirements, scope and progress.

Refer to the Nine Crucial Capabilities

In the long history of humankind those who learned to collaborate
and improvise most effectively have prevailed.

Charles Darwin

Introduction

A project is undertaken by a range of players, each one having a part to play in the venture – sometime, part-time or full-time. As stakeholders and sometimes players, they distinguish themselves by their particular interests, responsibilities and the contributions that they each make to the venture.

Their roles can be positioned across a range or continuum. At one end we can place the stakeholders who are prominent as players, actively sharing a collective responsibility for the management of their project. At the other end are stakeholders who do not involve themselves directly in its management. These might include suppliers of materials, programme authorities, funding sources and regulators. But all stakeholders have a place on this continuum; their position depending on the nature of their interests and the extent to which they are involved in its management.

Much consideration is given to information systems that support a project and the measurement and control of its progress. But they are not a primary interest to this book. Instead we look here at the resolve, dialogue and organisation of a project regime, i.e. how the players conduct themselves in the venture and how they manage its pace of progress (see Chapter 6).

The book examines, explores and suggests ways to recognise the beneficial behaviours of organisations (or 'project regimes'), that are now achieving strong project management capability and that are reaching high levels of maturity.

The challenge for a project regime is to orchestrate and accommodate contributions and to resolve issues expressed by stakeholders; each holding different views of the world. It has to continually review the project's goals as well as the ways in which it intends to realise their value.

So in managing a project, the issue of collaboration is central. And this is always true: not only during those testing and confusing times when the need for greater orderliness might be most apparent. Collaboration is an enduring imperative. It occurs as joint action between groups of players and is enabled by their social interaction. It is a key feature of all project management activities and is a test of their efficacy. Collaboration can be seen as 'a network of commitments' (Winograd and Flores, 1987: 150) and this definition serves to emphasise the players' commitment as crucial. In 'Towards a holding environment: Building shared understanding and commitment in projects' (Culmsee and Awati, 2012), the authors offer the principle that collaboration is something that depends fundamentally on its participants acquiring:

- a shared understanding of project goals … that leads to

- a shared commitment to achieve them.

Project collaboration depends on meeting these conditions; this often presenting a significant challenge. The regime must ensure a common understanding of its goals and secure both the individual and collective commitments of its players.

Rich dialogue is required for engagement and reflection. Dialogue provides opportunities for stakeholders to explore, learn and reason their case and to comprehend and consider those of others. Initial positions need to be openly scrutinised and then ways found for reconciliation and agreement. As a group they will depend on a strong Engagement Capability (see Chapter 4).

Problems in accomplishing collaboration in the management of a project are not uncommon and can become the Achilles heel to achieving progress. Stratagems are needed that are capable of shifting the perspectives of stakeholders away from entrenched positions, defensiveness or scepticism and towards maintaining greater confidence in the venture and its protagonists.

Stratagems and methods for a project to acquire the shared understanding and commitment needed for collaboration, are examined in Chapter 4, 'Connections'.

The Single-Minded Project

The following story offers some clues as to how groups of project players can become more productive and creative. Readers are invited to consider Janet's experience in managing a project 'single-handedly' and reflect on the patterns of her thinking and decision-making.

Janet has committed herself on a Saturday morning to prepare a special Sunday lunch to be held the following day for her extended family and friends. This requires catering for 14 people. The period of notice is short, as is the floor-space and the situation features complexity and uncertainty. She recognises that the project will be managed 'live'; continuously and in its entirety in her own single mind: from the decision to proceed, through to its conclusion and the washing of the dishes.

Using her single mind, Janet has to embrace all matters concerning the Sunday Lunch Project. Its planning, products, resources, quality issues, priorities, interests, processes and dependencies will all be continually scanned, scrutinised and acted upon by Janet. She does this, so far as we know, in a way that can only be accomplished using the instrument we know as the human mind.

It is late Saturday afternoon when Janet learns for the first time that three of her guests are vegetarians, and she then also realises that her dining room will be too small to seat everyone in comfort. She must seek more spacious accommodation for the party. Janet is able to take all this in her stride. In her mind – that single, interconnected processor – she is sensing, imagining, scoping, executing, re-scoping and re-planning. Dependencies, consequences and trade-offs are all recognised, considered and acted upon at every stage of the Sunday Lunch Project's life-cycle.

This facility of a single mind confers major advantages over a project undertaken by a group of minds. It has the capacity to consider all options and to be aware of all known constraints; to be conscious of all that is happening within a context; to recognise all dependencies; to scrutinise the amalgamation of factors and judge trade-offs.

A crucial question that we have to ask is whether a regular project management regime consisting of many minds, can expect to emulate the same 'single-mindedness' as was available to Janet when she managed the Sunday Lunch Project.

The high levels of social engagement required for a group to achieve single-mindedness depend on members of a group each having a strong sense of self and social awareness, a belief in the project's methods and purpose, curiosity, a sense of order and pace, connection and the skills needed to reconcile competing and contrasting interests. These so-called 'soft skills' are now recognised by today's more successful and mature enterprises as the 'hard ground' on which strong connection and performance rests. It is a base-line that can sustain a project regime to be responsive, reliable and adaptable than those of its competitors.

Some organisations are now experiencing a 'Venture Shift' (see Figure 1.1 on the opposite page), challenging them to reach away from a prescribed or 'traditional venture' mode towards one that can function in 'high venture'; where it will be more adaptive and agile and even 'extreme' in its irregularity and where the risks (and opportunities) are likely to be greater. Competition demands it. Many project regimes, in having to embrace the emergent and demanding issues of a project, now recognise that they must develop a response capability that is rapid and sure-footed. They need to be able to sense issues earlier, be more discerning and acting more promptly. The risks are greatest in circumstances that are 'high venture'; this obliging the regime to become more functionally reliable.

If project players can work together as 'a single mind' they should surely expect to emulate some of Janet's capacity to respond more reliably to events. But how can this be achieved? There is a powerful ambiguity here that will not have escaped readers. While 'single mindedness' is shown here to be about a group of players acting as one, the expression has another more familiar and equally vital meaning. This lies in the determination, will and tenacity of the players. We are speaking here of the strength of a conviction to succeed in an endeavour, through the abilities and dispositions that this requires. Managing

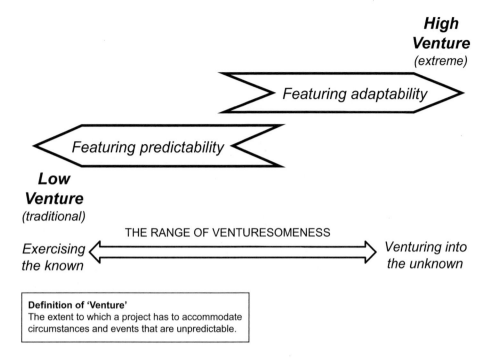

Figure 1.1   The Venture of a Project Regime
Source: 2012 © EngagementWorks Ltd.

a project is characterised by uncertainty and that requires a project regime's dedication to endure. This vital attribute is referred to here as 'Resolute Leadership' (see Chapter 3).

Alliancing at the Andrew Field

This project developed and commissioned a platform and undersea facilities to extract oil from under the North Sea in the 1990s. As a recognised example of 'alliancing', Andrew qualifies as a 'single-minded project' from its capacity to maximise its pace of progress, reliability of execution and the quality of the players' social engagement and collaboration.

The owner, BP, and its contractors committed from the outset to share the commercial risks of the project: to share any losses of their venture as well as to share any surplus or savings (a form of contract sometimes referred to as 'Gain and Pain Share'). This exceptional example of collaboration between the rig's contractors and BP led to the abolition of task duplication and other restrictive practices then endemic to the oil and gas extraction industry. The result was very significant cost savings from the original target estimate and these were shared as profit that was shared. Delivery was six months early and, exceptionally for the oil and gas extraction sector, there were no legal claims made on the contract on its completion (Sakal, 2005).

> *Once we realised that the historic tiers of authority, cross checking and approval were gone – that we were no longer waiting for permission – we grasped the freedom with relish (Bill Ebon of Brown and Root).*

Here, Bill Ebon, a manager with a major contractor, remarks upon BP's decision to 'partner behaviour with technology' as the key to a venture that would otherwise not have been commercially viable. He was referring to the adoption of a radically different project regime in which BP managers and engineers worked in close collaboration, sharing their common objectives. It was a major departure from traditional adversarial working practices in the oil industry (Knott, 1996). The players in this project are quoted as saying:

> *Co-operation between alliance members made innovation possible.*

> *Having an open dialogue with the fabricators, we discovered what they really needed from us as designers.*

> *We're proud of our work in every job, but there was something extra on Andrew, an extra degree of trust.*

> *Company identity, who worked for what company, became almost irrelevant to us and largely indistinguishable to the outside observer.*

> *The Andrew project exhibited high ideals in its early meetings between BP and the contractors; but we suspected that in time, matters would revert to traditional business as usual. But not so (Knott, 1996: 14, 15, 42, 140–45).*

The era of large field operations was at that time giving way to the development and exploitation of smaller fields in which margins were squeezed. Development costs and the cost of manpower would have to be substantially reduced. Colin Maclean, then manager of programmes at BP Exploration, observed:

> *At this stage, the method for achieving these goals was not apparent and we realised that we could not rely on our past experience.*

For these reasons the Andrew Field had earlier been found to be commercially unattractive. But BP decided that it should have a flagship with which to prove a new approach to capital investment. It also realised that the commercial arrangements with engineering contractors needed to become more effective as well as more efficient. It was decided that an integrated approach was needed that would radically change the working practices of BP's staff in working with those of the contractors.

A small preliminary development team was formed to set off on this track. Paul Bobby, one of BP's project co-ordinators, reported that:

> We had never experienced this degree of integration before. Once the old barriers to openness and clarity were broken down, the resulting dialogue and understanding gave us the opportunity to determine the real cost drivers on the project.

It was Bobby's team that first placed value on the advantages of collaboration. They successfully established the foundations for a progressive project community in which behaviour was focused on the project's technical and financial success. From this, a strong and professional ethos developed. The project was delivered six months early and at a final cost of £290 million. The original BP estimate had been £450 million. The 'go-ahead estimate' prepared at the pre-contract stage by what was termed the 'concerted body' (BP with representatives of its main contractors) was £393 million. The saving of £103 million was over 26 per cent of the estimate made at go-ahead.

The story of Andrew is related in *No Business as Usual*, a book by Terry Knott, an oil industry journalist (Knott, 1996). It describes the development and operation of a high-performing work organisation. The engineers and technicians deployed hitherto were accustomed to a traditional contract working regime in which trust was explicitly excluded from the manning of tasks and the transactions that arranged them. Legal matters and contractual terms dominated the choices and working practices. These would encourage delay, excessive quality control, duplication of resources, poor co-ordination and extension claims. It was these behaviours that piled on the costs and in this project, they were largely removed.

From the outset, it was recognised that the project would require a different approach to the assessment and selection of contractors. The executives nominated by contractors to undertake work were assessed for their professional attitude and approach to joint working. BP knew that success depended on close social engagement between the players and collaboration between groups. At the pre-contract stage, these managers were pre-qualified as suitable for Alliance Working. As part of the tendering process, if a contractor was unable to nominate a manager who could be recognised by BP as suited to working in this way, their tender was rejected.

Sir John Browne, then the chief executive of BP, put the achievement into some perspective:

> ... *relationships have been built to the mutual advantage of everyone involved. The savings in capital costs and the early production of oil are major achievements in the drive toward transforming the efficiency and the profitability of our business (Knott, 1996: 160).*

Before the Andrew project, such behaviours did not feature in BP's culture. But it is evident that as the project developed, genuine candour, higher levels of confidence, energy and a stronger acceptance of the obligations between players developed. Responsibility was widely devolved in BP's organisation, in those of contractors and in their joint working. It was behaviour that mirrored the working practices that developed in the Rocky Flats project in Colorado (see Chapter 9). A fuller account of project alliancing is set out in 'Project Alliancing' (Sakal, 2005).

So what can be learned from how the project regime on the Andrew Field project produced such outstanding results? Perhaps most significantly it was BP's commitment to Project Alliancing, initiated through contracting and maturing into the maxim 'Single Team – not enough; it's Total Team'. Through these arrangements the project players shared a common purpose out of which emerged their willing commitment to deliver the project's goals.

Many surveys and books have been written about how projects fail. Instead, this is an account of how a project came to be successful.

Apple Inc. and a Different Formula for Collaboration

Some exceptionally successful projects were undertaken under the leadership of Steve Jobs at Apple Inc. He was often strongly critical of Apple's project players (Levy, 2006) and this behaviour came from his insistence on a particular approach; demanding the pursuit of his own vision for products and his way of doing business. The term 'reality distortion field' (RDF) was coined by staff to describe the regime under Jobs' leadership. Jobs' point of view and practices continually challenged conventional wisdom and what others would claim as reality. As Levy relates, Jobs was 'often at odds with the facts', but his ethos was nevertheless irresistible to many working with him. As Levy relates:

> *On the one hand the term RDF reflected the frustration of Mac workers; Jobs would get things into his head and that would be it. Only a repeated assault by the experience of actual reality (when things just didn't work) would change his position. But the term was not strictly pejorative. Jobs was often right and only his unwillingness to compromise would convince others that taking an un-trodden path was correct. More to the point, people who were in range of the reality distortion field often came to believe that they could actually accomplish what seemed to be impossible (Levy, 2006: 227–8).*

Steve Jobs created and successfully presided over a community of people who largely shared common values, common ways of thinking, productive conversation and synergy – albeit it would be wrong to suppose that consensus often ruled. But collaboration did. Very many of the players were passionately loyal to him and while it was far from typical as a project community (is there such a thing?), it was a remarkable demonstration of the value of social capital and the exploitation of diversity. The strength of a professional project management regime and community arises from its resolve, its values, beliefs and behaviours. In every project, such features uniquely combine to produce a project regime behaving and performing in its own distinctive way.

Apple launched the iPod in October 2001. Rather than a technological breakthrough, it was a shrewd combination of existing components, including a miniature hard drive from Toshiba and a battery from Sony. In an eight-month 'project sprint', the people at Apple engaged and collaborated within and between its businesses, resolving a range of complex problems and issues. The project required countless interactions between design, hardware, manufacturing, marketing, software and external suppliers.

Until this time, Sony had been the dominant global player in portable music players, in the wake of its highly successful Walkman. But Sony experienced fundamental difficulties in competing with Apple and its iPod. When their 'Connect' product was launched in May 2004, Walt Mossberg of the influential *Wall Street Journal* wrote, 'Until Sony fixes the multitude of sins in this product, steer clear of it'. In April 2007, Apple sold its 100 millionth iPod, and by August of that year Sony had withdrawn 'Connect' from the market.

The Sony project had been dogged by its own organisation's hyper-competitive culture and territorial rivalry. Engineers working in Sony Corporation businesses in the US and Japan were encouraged to 'out-do' one another rather than to engage and collaborate. Sony fell into a trap of their own making when they supposed that the necessary collaboration would be available within and between these rival territories. When the ironically named 'Connect' project came along, depending as it did on collaboration more than newly developed technology, the decentralised Sony Corporation found itself hopelessly hobbled in a struggle to achieve competitive advantage. The story is reported by Morten T. Hansen (2009).

Collaboration Arises Locally

Social engagement and collaboration showed themselves as distinctive and valuable qualities of Apple's project management under Steve Jobs. His form of engagement and collaboration was extraordinary but highly effective in the behaviours that it engendered and the innovation and pace of progress that was achieved. A comparison of the arrangements made here by Jobs with those adopted on the Andrew Field indicates that any collaborative regime has to be devised and configured locally and cannot be derived from a formula prescribed from elsewhere.

In the growing 'projectisation' of business and public sector organisations, many project regimes are led or sponsored by senior managers with little experience of the management of projects. An understanding of how to equip an organisation to be methodical and collaborative and the skills needed to achieve this kind of conduct are critical. Ill-informed decision-making can not only blight a project; it will also delay the development and maturing of a project regime. Perhaps if sponsors and other seniors and executives were involved more closely in undertaking the management of a project, a more successful partnership would develop with project management colleagues.

Shaping a Project

In the foreword to *Industrial Megaprojects*, James B. Porter Jr, chief engineer and former vice president, Engineering and Operations of DuPont, has this to say:

> *After more than 40 years working in the capital project arena, I remain mystified by the extreme reluctance of very intelligent business and*

technical leaders to validate past experience. It is my opinion that failing to accept that there are best project concepts, when executed in a disciplines manner, deliver predictably good results ... makes no business sense. Over the course of my career I have struggled to find the best way of communicating this and to show that the business value was so obvious, that the use of proven approaches should be a no-brainer. I had begun to fear that we were all destined to continue to validate the observation expressed in this quote from Douglas Adams, the English humourist and science fiction novelist:

Human beings, who are almost unique in having the ability to learn from the experience of others, are remarkable for their apparent disinclination to do so (Merrow, 2011: ix).

Project management is not the routine that some perceive it to be. Any project's path of progress is strewn with fresh realisations, unexpected events and innovation. These are inherent features; obliging players to engage and re-engage, collaborate and sense issues promptly; then to set a new course while sharing planning activities that they know will be continually revised.

In the preparation work prior to a project's launch date, a project's foundations have to be laid with some care. In his blog 'Shaping Sound Projects' (Smith, 2010), Charles Smith describes 'Project Formation' through 'Shaping'. Through his Six Element Framework, Smith sees projects as complex social enterprises that are commonly exposed to:

- control measures that inhibit players' inventiveness;

- the interests and ambitions of players in groups ('tribal' impact);

- the dissemination of procedures and routines to enact a tactic or standard;

- project players working within a project regime to pursue goals unrelated to the project's planned outputs/outcomes;

- events that prompt or lead to reframing the purpose or progress of a project (Smith refers to this as 'peripety');

- a player's behaviour that is driven by personal volition serving allegiances or ambitions.

Shaping as a regular feature of project management is too often neglected. It serves the need to establish and sustain a stable platform from which to initiate and develop a successful venture. Edward W. Merrow, in his book *Industrial Megaprojects* (2011), defines project management as 'the science of project planning combined with the art of reacting to surprises during execution'. Alleviating the incidence and impact of surprises is an objective of shaping. As such, it has a crucial part to play in a project's management of risk.

Merrow provides these five headings to prompt likely issues in shaping a project as undertaken in the oil and gas sector:

1.   Understanding the context.

2.   Assessing the potential for creating value.

3.   Assessing comparative advantages of objectives.

4.   Identifying and understanding the stakeholders.

5.   Thinking about partners.

Professional Pointers

•   The issue of collaboration lies centre stage.

•   Collaboration can be seen as 'a network of commitments'.

•   A shared understanding of project goals and a shared commitment are keys to collaboration.

•   Rich and sincere dialogue is needed for a project's engagement and reflection.

•   Players acting in concert when single-minded, can expect to be more resolute, engaged and ready to respond.

•   The will, candour and tenacity of the players.

•   'We were no longer waiting for permission – we grasped the freedom with relish'.

- 'Company identity; who worked for what company, became almost irrelevant to us and largely indistinguishable to the outside observer'.

- 'Single Team is not enough; it's Total Team'.

- 'Human beings, who are almost unique in having the ability to learn from the experience of others, are remarkable for their apparent disinclination to do so'.

References

Culmsee, P. and Awati, C. (2012). Towards a holding environment: Building shared understanding and commitment in projects. *International Journal of Managing Projects in Business*, 5(3): 528–48.

Hansen, M.T. *Collaboration: How Leaders Avoid the Traps, Create Unity, and Reap Big Results*. Cambridge, MA: Harvard Business Press.

Knott, T. (1996). *No Business as Usual: An Extraordinary North Sea Result*. London: British Petroleum.

Levy, S. (2006). *The Perfect Thing: How the iPod Shuffles Commerce, Culture, and Coolness*. London: Random House.

Merrrow, E.W. (2011). *Industrial Megaprojects: Concepts, Strategies, and Practices for Success*. Hoboken, NJ: Wiley.

PMI [Hunsberger, K.] (2007). Finding closure. *PM Network*, January, 31–6. Available at: http://www.pmi.org/About-Us/Our-Professional-Awards/~/media/PDF/Awards/PMN0107_Rockyflats.ashx [accessed 7 May 2014].

Sakal, M.A. (2005). Project alliancing: A relational contracting mechanism for dynamic projects. *Lean Construction Journal*, 2(1): 67–78.

Smith, C. (2010). *Shaping Sound Projects*. Wellingtone Project Management. Available at: http://www.wellingtone.co.uk/blog/?p=114 [accessed 15 April 2013].

Winograd, T. and Flores, F. (1987). *Understanding Computers and Cognition: A New Foundation for Design*. Norwood, NJ: Ablex.

Chapter 2
A Project's Able People

*Contributing as Competent, Lucid and Committed
Project Players*

Working with rigour and enterprise. Relying on their experience and social engagement to resolve professional, social, organisational and domain issues.

Refer to the Nine Crucial Capabilities

Introduction

Susceptibility to the uncertainties, complexity and ambiguity of project management must make it a prime contender as one of the most demanding of occupations. For those who thrive on and can be robust to such a working environment and the leadership that it constantly requires, it is fascinating work and can be immensely fulfilling.

While firmly dependent on systematic principles and methods, the essential competence and capabilities that are needed rely strongly on experiential learning, curiosity and an appetite for venture. The ability of players also relies on an understanding of many matters lying beyond project management, as it is now commonly recognised as a management discipline.

As a capability that is crucial to industry, civic bodies, government and NGOs, its practitioners too often find themselves disconnected from a career mainstream – something that is more readily available to such disciplines as engineering, general management, IT, technology and accounting. The supply of talented, experienced and professional people needed at high levels is sometimes prejudiced in this way.

The complexity and innovation-hungry project regime depends on the leadership of practitioners at every level. While seniority and hierarchy are relied upon for coherence and order, this protocol must not be allowed to inhibit the engagement and the high expectations of players.

The Value of Professional Experience

Able project professionals are generally well educated and practised in the principles, methods and behaviours of project management. But there are talented professionals who have something more to offer. When we experience their behaviour, it becomes apparent that they are applying recognised project management practices, but often without these being explicit.

For these players, much of their professional ability has become self-evident or tacit: integrated and retained as heuristics in the form of 'rules of thumb' or 'common sense' (Hillson and Murray-Webster, 2005). This can be readily understood from the Japanese principle of 'Shu Ha Ri' (Cockburn, 2006) in which the most accomplished professionals or 'masters', without appearing to be conscious of key processes and principles, can nevertheless be seen to apply them implicitly and with great skill.

A powerful analogy is cast by Lesley Prince, expressed in the title of his paper 'Eating the menu rather than the dinner: Tao and leadership' (Prince, 2008). He argues that choices are in practice exercised by players who do not consciously 'over-think' about what they do: they simply make the decisions as they observe them to be required – responding with ease to situations as they are encountered. He observes that many of the factors that must be taken into account in the evaluation and resolution of problems have, as a result of their familiarity, become integrated into regular conduct.

Consider the behaviour of a tennis player. All that is involved in deciding a stroke of the ball – the distance, the angle, the body position, the potential forced error, the position of the other player on the court, and then the power and direction of the shot – cannot be consciously planned before the stroke is played. But for the accomplished player it *is* planned and in a moment. Experiences are fed into the mind together with the player's observations;

for the player to then unconsciously decide how their return stroke is to be played.

Resolving project issues can be problematic and players cannot expect complex and unique situations and their dynamics to always be completely understood, even in retrospect. Different people witnessing the same social situation will observe it, remember it, learn from it and report it – differently. It is for this reason that 'lessons learned', recorded and then made accessible for use at some future time and place cannot be expected to capture, store and subsequently and usefully make a behaviour scenario available at a future date. An experience cannot be communicated.

For any organisation, systematising 'Information Management' is important; but as a means of identifying and accumulating knowledge and behaviour acquired from people's experience it has, as early exponents of knowledge management discovered, significant limitations. In an attempt to gather and retain new ideas and knowledge of useful and emergent practice, some enterprises have established groups known as Communities of Practice (CoP). Members share an enthusiasm and interest in a specialism and then commit to contributing to its enrichment: making a 'live' learning resource available. The expectation is that fresh knowledge will be collected, scrutinised, defined and retained by an expert group's collective consciousness, acting as curator – to then make this ready to be shared with other parties via a dialogue.

Communities of Practice are commonly developed on a basis first described by Etienne Wenger (Wenger, 1998). Their application is described by Hubert Saint-Onge and Debra Wallace in their book Leveraging Communities of Practice for Strategic Advantage (2003). The Project Management Institute (PMI) has adopted the idea to facilitate its members working together in the development of project management practices.

But prescriptions in the form of standards and defined methods are only one aspect of capability. It may be that universal and conscious algorithms of behaviour will one day be available to us, but that possibility cannot deny us now of the opportunities to play our best shot with what we have. It is perhaps why many professionals emphasise the value of people's 'experience', without defining it with any exactness, the abilities that are supposed. A true measure of a player's capability lies in their capacity to connect concurrently with principles, training, past experience, methodical rigour, assessment of a situation, engagement with fellow professionals and the critical choices to be addressed.

An Ability to Handle Complexity

Managing and leading projects of complexity and uncertainty is demanding and potentially stressful. It tests the value of a professional's prior experience and what has been learned from it, to enhance their expertise. In the case of project and programme management, the range of abilities required across all fields of human endeavour can be greater than that required in most other disciplines.

The ambitious new Willy Brandt Berlin Airport was conceived in 2002 and intended as a glittering symbol of the city's importance as a global hub. As this is being written, yet another delay takes completion potentially deep into 2014. The story of this project offers important lessons; contrasting public and private sector project management capability and potential. It can also be read as a fable; illustrating the significance of players' and stakeholders' motives, political adroitness and their capacity to handle complexity.

The opening event, originally set for 2007 at a total cost of €1.2 billion, was passed and another date set for June 2012. This was then postponed again until March 2013, when it was cancelled yet again and has now been pushed back to 2014. However, no specific opening date has been announced.

Officials cite numerous technical and budgetary problems that have delayed the airport's construction and fitting-out. The final cost is now estimated at more than €4 billion, or $5 billion. Berlin has become the butt of jokes across the country. 'Berlin – we can do everything, but nothing right' is the motto of some German media organisations.

The airport terminal in 2012 appeared complete but it stood empty, with very little activity apparent. Most of the project recovery work was being conducted elsewhere, where tasks were being re-scoped and remedial works were planned.

The programme management for the airport construction, conducted by public officials, has been exceptionally problematic, with claims that the decision made to dismiss the private sector contractor, two years into a 50-year contract, was the biggest of many mistakes.

As reported in *Der Spiegel* (Berg, 2012) in November 2012:

> *There are good reasons for the fact that the public sector often struggles with such large-scale projects. For one thing, elected officials are*

not responsible to investors but to their electorate. They have to act transparently, involve citizens, manage the money and solve complex infrastructure issues.

New public buildings have reached a level of complexity that is apparently too much for state officials to handle. Slimmed-down administrations are hardly capable of controlling construction projects. Their resources are easily overwhelmed by the complicated interplay of technical, financial and scheduling plans. And heads of governments also lack the time to manage effectively and supervise a complex construction project.

'The public sector must take its function as builder more seriously', says Felix Pakleppa, the managing director of the German Construction Federation. Companies need legitimate budgets and reliable planning, he explains. 'Many administrations simply lack the experts needed to manage complex construction projects', he said.

This account of a calamitous failure of programme management raises fundamental questions about the risks that accompany the appointment of inexperienced people to manage large and complex ventures. It prompts questions as to how and why they were appointed, as well as about their competence. Even aside from political factors, programmes of this nature will inevitably struggle in Donald Schön's 'swampy lowlands' (Schön, 1983).

When confronted with the challenges of managing such a programme, an experienced professional on their arrival, will observe, learn and infer from the copious accounts that they hear and the patterns of events that they observe: factors that are likely to be less clear to the inexperienced. Such insight provides them with an ability to apply trade-offs, leverage relationships, question working assumptions, assess the ability of professional players, judge the nature of risks and through their professional networks know the views, interests and opinions of experienced observers and stakeholders. In anticipation of likely events and decisions, they will be quickly and actively be considering alternative options to those then running or being planned.

The choices available to them, compared to the options available to less experienced officials and commentators, will afford them greater discretion and influence over how and when problems can be resolved or averted and progress made. Their judgements can be expected to be more reliable in deciding on the appointment and deployment of people and when necessary, in out-placing people away from situations that have become for them unsustainable.

The Loss of Prime Contractor Expertise

The headcount of personnel employed on a project often includes contractors whose time is purchased for their skills and expertise; often for a limited period. They are not included on the payroll but are paid under a contract for services and probably provided by a third-party agency. Sometimes they will be employed by an outsource supplier to provide a service or a function as a component part of a main contractor's project organisation.

The extent of such arrangements has recently grown substantially, often in pursuit of a main contractor's policy that seeks to limit the range of their company's capability or to provide specialist expertise that they have, for reasons of economy, decided to exclude from their skills inventory.

The instances of outsourcing are common in larger projects. The arrangements are also intended to satisfy a peak or temporary labour demand or are adopted as a strategy to retain only those specialist functions needed to ensure the retention of core competencies (Prahalad and Hamel, 1990). The remaining functions and expertise not required to differentiate the firm but nevertheless required by particular projects, are then provided by contractors or outsourced. But this in some sectors has led to unintended consequences.

In *Industrial Megaprojects*, Edward Merrow explains some of the long-term impacts of contracting and outsourcing as this has been exercised over the last 30 years. Main contractors have sought to 'run lean' to minimise base costs, but this has sometimes also increased the risks of error, poor integration of activities, disconnection with supply chains and weaknesses in the recruitment, training and development of professionals. These issues are today presenting major problems to engineering and project management. Merrow states:

> *The most important problem created by weakness in the owner project cardre is internal coherence. The owner project teams glue the owner functions together to make a project capability coherent. Without some group to perform that essential function, the high level of internal cooperation necessary to generate a successful megaproject cannot be mustered. Most companies cannot even get feedback from Operations to Engineering about what aspects of design were poor, because operations*

do not have the time to be bothered and no one cares anymore about the
long-term health of the company and its assets (Merrow, 2011: 129).

Perhaps the key question is to ask where the savings in manpower costs of a lean policy become outweighed by the costs of rework, redesign, delay and a business's credibility and future. In applying a lean strategy, practitioners sometimes fail to experience or refine their ability to ensure collaboration. Ongoing project management maturity is held up or goes into reverse.

Career Risks for Professionals

A project professional, in pursuing their career, will seek recognition and reward for their achievement and progress. But they should be aware that the path of a project management career is often lined with risks implicit to its occupational circumstances and their politics. Factors governing the fortunes of a project professional can run independently of their own choices and actions. While project management outcomes are very often attributable to a tangle of causes and behaviours, the patterns as observed and interpreted by some can lead to the award of personal credit or blame that is subjective, controversial and that is sometimes unwarranted.

When considering whether to accept an invitation to manage a project, a project management professional will naturally seek to anticipate likely opportunities and challenges. They will in some way pursue a risk assessment. They will scope the requirement and its shape and sketch out a project plan for themselves: assessing the ability and circumstances of the sponsor and stakeholders to assess the chances of building and deploying a regime capable of delivering the project's promises. They will consider whether, in their execution of the work, an error or even a failure as judged by the prevailing culture, would be likely to threaten their standing or reputation.

The greatest prizes go to those who have greater ability, confidence and enterprise (and luck) to conduct project work successfully and to handle risk and risk attitude (Hillson and Murray-Webster, 2005). When a professional is expected to walk the tight-rope of complexity or uncertainty, 'air cover' is often necessary from the sponsor. An enterprise depends on its most able people being willing to accept the risks associated with the management of challenging projects. Senior managers must either mitigate the risks to a professional or be sufficiently generous in their rewards and security provisions to attract able people, despite the risks of difficulty or failure. Unfortunately, project managers are often casualties of this as a phenomenon. This can be the result of misunderstanding, a failure of rapport between a project manager and their steering group or other hosting authority.

Able players in developing as professional leaders need their development to be robust to exercise a range of responsibilities that involve:

- Continual involvement with customers, users and other stakeholders.

- Managing the pace of progress (see Chapter 6) to manage and communicate project health.

- Demanding and adversarial situations.

- Building relationships with influential figures.

- Exercising responsibility, influence and leadership.

- Exercising power and authority.

- Providing and obtaining regular mentoring.

- Taking responsibility for execution and for the work of other players.

- The assurance from the scrutiny of their seniors and line executives.

It was more common in the past for able professionals to have some confidence that their career security would be underwritten by their employer. Such a feeling of security engendered in this way has however for many reasons in recent years, become less common. The implications for a professional's sense of career risk have been profound. Not all employers have recognised the extent to which insecurity amongst project management professionals has limited their managers' commitment to the enterprise and the management of risk on which their business depends.

The CEO of a software business once suggested to the writer that before concluding the assessment of a newcomer's suitability for the role of project manager, it is necessary to wait for the results of their third project. In their first, objectives will be achieved despite the debris and delay, overspend and strained relationships. They will be determined to succeed and work all hours to do so. In their second project that achievement can have brought a false confidence, with the result that there can be a calamity. His theory closed in claiming that these experiences make it possible for a more authentic indication of ability after an appraisal on the completion of the third project.

Another story is related by a very experienced programme director. He had successfully completed the installation of a very large telecommunications network that involved an elaborate and complex execution phase. In his performance review with a director of his firm, he made it known that he was very pleased with his project's success. His boss was prompted to say, 'Well it's true that this was a great job well done. But I wonder whether you had realised that we had assigned to you an "A Team". We'll understand your capability better in managing your next job when I think we will assign a "B Team"!'

'The Project Team': An Abiding Myth

Have you noticed the preference that groups sometimes display in their need to be seen as a team? In recent years the term has shifted in its meaning from being a specific reference to a group committed to single common and coherent purpose, to one that can label any organisation. It may be that the habit of using of the term 'project team' is sometimes a mistake when used in this general way as it can devalue the equally important contribution that we expect from people acting in an individual capacity.

A popular definition of a team is 'a small number of people with complementary skills who are committed to a common purpose, set of performance goals, and approach for which they hold themselves mutually accountable' (Katzenbach and Smith, 1993: 45).

A town council in Britain recently referred to itself as a team. A council must manage multiple priorities, interests, relationships, personal and party ambitions and controversies. Councillors who represent competing interests and the needs of voters, government and statutory bodies are accommodated. This makes council goals sometimes contradictory, unpredictable and often ambiguous. Members struggle to make one another mutually accountable. Activities are multifaceted, complex and irregular. To see a town council as a team is to misunderstand its purpose and function.

So this definition of a team (on the previous page) indicates a unity and coherence that in the case of a town council simply does not apply. If instead we consider the conduct of a town refuse-collection crew in gathering domestic waste and disposing of it, there is more of a common purpose. Conduct is regular and coherent and the crew can be suitably referred to as a team. Irregularity is clearly greater in the council organisation than it is for those deployed and dedicated to refuse collection.

So where does a 'project team' fall in this range of irregularity? A project manager, in resourcing the venture, has to ensure that there are able people who represent the interests and goals in play and are together capable of doing the work. But does 'team' behaviour adequately describe the undercurrents, delegated responsibilities, dynamics and dilemmas of project work?

Any project group must perform many functions besides that of sharing the overriding 'committing to a common purpose'. Some of the players represent vested interests in the project, and these often find themselves competing or in opposition. The struggle is to achieve connected autonomy; a feature of an organisation that can link and co-ordinate the separate endeavours on which a project's overall success relies.

A Project Regime

So practitioners need to decide whether the term 'project team' is sufficiently representative of the work and purpose of a project organisation's players. The best term to apply should resonate with the characteristic behaviours and transactions of project management where, as well as functioning as a team, must also accommodate a mixture of interests, opposing values and behaviours, controversy and internal negotiation. It must also be capable of a degree of autonomy. 'Regime' is here used as a more suitable and robust term for an organisation that must allow autonomy of its sub-groups. It must assert its own direction and endeavour; continually responding to events to configure itself to secure and sustain routes to delivery that are fit for purpose.

In support of the term 'regime', readers will note that while the expression has in the past been reserved for authoritarian political formations, it is now commonly used as a label for more benevolent ventures: for example a 'fitness regime', 'hygiene regime, 'quality management regime', 'traffic regime', 'procurement regime', 'manufacturing regime' 'health regime' and 'study regime'.

Adversity and Our Resilience to It

We all hope for a positive outcome from every project decision, but we can never predict their impact with certainty. No matter how comprehensive our preparation and planning is made to be, we cannot know, prior to their application, what the outcomes or their consequences will be.

Goals must be sustained by a strong element of optimism. Subsequent events as they play out through the project are likely to challenge earlier assumptions and can thereby strengthen or weaken our progress and even our resolve. A project management professional must face the trials of adversity and learn to accept them with equanimity. It is an experience that is implicit to the role. So much depends upon the strength of resolve and in refining the balance between a project as a risk enterprise and as a prescribed endeavour (NAO, 2013), the professional support from fellow-players and their level-headedness.

Only after the passage of time can the value of a project decision be usefully evaluated. Moreover, for projects featuring complex patterns of interdependence, the attribution of achievement to players and shareholders can be complex and controversial – dependent on the maturity of a project regime, its community and the strength of its Cultural Anchor (see Chapter 4).

We all seek to minimise the risk of delay and disappointment, but uncertainty is a project's constant companion. So how should we sensibly proceed? Part of the answer is that old saw 'experience': the richness of it, rather than the years of it. In any project work, there is a 'mess' of disorder, controversy, dilemmas, interference, rival interests, misunderstandings and problem-solving as well as more ordered conduct. The most accomplished players make the most sense out of this; respecting those circumstances that call for a 'loose-tight' approach (see Chapter 7).

A project has been referred to as an 'improbability made to work'. It involves situations in which interactions between people both within and between groups are crucial to progress. The quality of professional ability, social engagement, collaboration and governance determines whether matters are resolved or are allowed to weaken the pace of progress.

The next to greatest talent of a project professional is to make decisions with a better than average hit-rate. But the greatest talent lies in the capacity to learn from the decisions already made, to understand their impact and to then be equipped to redeploy them. Decisions have to be made mindful of possibilities, the weight of interests and the capacity of players and their regime to execute them. The most able project managers draw on their experience, take notice of and characterise patterns of behaviour and insight and then store them consciously or unconsciously – later to inform and sustain their decision-making and their counsel to others.

Stay Cool

It can get scary when the unexpected happens. For a moment at least, players might feel that they are losing control. Their blood supply heads for the muscles of their arms and legs – to flee or to fend off a physical threat that isn't there. Fight or flight is an instinctive response to what we see as an immediate threat. We feel an automatic reaction. This may be OK for outrunning sabre-tooth tigers, but it is less useful when played out in front of other project players, sponsors, users and customers in the lead-up to a critical decision. We must equip ourselves to be emotionally robust and avoid becoming a victim of the moment.

We get to feel a lot better when we are able to learn more about the situation and share this with other players. Remember that old boss of yours and her response when she was faced with a predicament like this? She didn't miss a beat! Maybe you didn't know then that this was not her first encounter in Death Valley! She stayed in control and was able to disguise her emotion. She might even have been able to redirect some of her blood supply to her brain where the need was greatest.

And people can get edgy when someone appears to be losing their way. There are better ways to share responses to the way that you feel. All projects have their moments, and a cool head is important – not only for resolving the problem but also for helping to keep other players' heads up. At such moments there is usually much more to learn about the situation and as someone once said, 'never lose the mask of relaxed brilliance'.

Project players have always to be prepared for the unexpected. Take a tip from the men who co-ordinate the arrival and departure of fighter jets from their positions on a carrier flight deck (Wagner, 2006). You don't want to be sucked into a jet intake, walk into an engine propeller, fall into an unprotected plane elevator or get blown overboard by a jet engine. All these things are possible and have happened, but instances are rare – surprisingly very rare. It looks to be the most hazardous place on earth ... but it isn't. Carrier deck teams are seen by US Navy psychologists to be working in a High Reliability Environment (HRE). Close attention is given to roles that are very clearly defined and to signalling by colour-coded clothing, using very animated hand signals and to the close engagement between team members. Orderliness can appear to be absent to the uninformed observer. Team members know their job and that of their team-mates, extremely well. They look out for each other and mess together, continually sharing their experiences. Safe practices are built on common values and habituated behaviour as well as from remaining alert and adaptable to surprises.

Like managing a flight deck, managing a project can be subjected to the unpredictable, and when opportunities present themselves, professionals need to inject order wherever and whenever they can. There can be good order and collaboration if people know what is expected of them, can anticipate some of the actions of other players, have the ability and tools to do the job and the opportunity to show their best and its potential. Groups must be kept aware of the big picture if they are to respond from connections within the regime. When this is the case, they can then expect to relish the 'craic' and exhilaration as they engage and collaborate. In such regimes, project issues and hazards show up on the radar early. And when issues do come your way, there's a better chance that the other players will respond to you in a concerted way.

Adversity Can Equip Us for More

Mark Seery, Assistant Professor of Psychology at the University at Buffalo, examined the suggestion that someone's prior experience that has involved them in a degree of personal adversity can equip them to become more resilient to further adversity. 'Our findings revealed', he says, 'that a history of some lifetime of adversity predicted lower distress, lower functional impairment and higher life satisfaction' (Seery, 2010).

The team also found that across this same sample, people with a history of lifetime adversity appeared less negatively affected by new instances of adversity than other players. Although these data cannot prove causation, Seery claims the evidence to be consistent with the proposition that, in moderation, regular exposure to adversity can contribute to an increase in resilience to it.

Two notable examples of project successes that might be partly explained by 'Adversity Resilience' come from the stories of Steve Jobs and Winston Churchill. Steve Jobs led the turnaround of Apple on his return to the organisation in 1996 following his expulsion by John Scully in 1985. When Steve Jobs returned to Apple, Michael Dell – whose company at that time sold more computers than any other – offered the following advice: 'I'd shut [Apple] down and give the money back to the shareholders' (Levy, 2006: 81). On resumption as CEO, Jobs led the radical and successful strategy away from competing directly with other PC manufacturers, taking the business into outstandingly successful product and marketing initiatives in music distribution, computer technology and mobile phone design.

Prior to World War Two, Winston Churchill's career was rich in experience and it was not without its struggles. He was blamed as a cabinet minister in 1915 for the defeat of the Royal Navy in its attempt to capture the Dardanelles from the Turks in World War One. Prior to this, in 1910 as Home Secretary, he deployed troops to restore order during a miners' strike in South Wales. Whilst such actions may have marked him down as a man who would do his utmost to maintain law and order, there were those who criticised his use of the military for actions that they felt should have been a matter for the police.

Later in his career, in 1940, when the Battle of Britain air battle was anticipated and the inventory of fighter aircraft was just 50 per cent of the expected requirement to defend Britain from invasion, Churchill appointed Lord Beaverbrook (Max Aitken, a journalist), as Minister for Aircraft Production – a politically controversial decision. This he did just two days after his appointment as Prime Minister. The move followed his message to the Air Ministry informing them that they were no longer responsible for aircraft production. Within eight weeks, the rate of supply of fighter aircraft had doubled.

Both these accounts suggest that professional ability and maturity will benefit from exacting and demanding experiences. Could it be that when someone feels their judgement might have failed them, that they can subsequently use that experience as a very personal and crucial learning opportunity? Such learning might then equip them to reflect with renewed clarity on the issues and the choices through which they had justified their decision. This in their subsequent decision-making might bring greater insight and confidence with which to resist a temptation to overlook or 'blind-side' important factors and to question the more 'obvious' options. This can be seen as an example of so-called 'reflective learning' (Schön, 1983).

And perhaps this explains why we often place value on people's prior experience over 'mere knowledge'. When project players find themselves presented with a complex situation they must exert themselves to the rigours of personal challenge as well as rational thinking, close engagement with other players, dialogue, cogent argument and emotional intelligence. This is where a resilience to adversity with its reflective learning, can serve a project player well.

Developing Proficient Players

Career paths in project management today, particularly for professionals working in less mature project regimes, often fail to offer the opportunities needed for the professional development of practitioners. The richness of experience at early career stages from working in a mature project management environment is critical.

Employers sometimes fall short of offering aspirant professional players the opportunities to witness the practices and behaviours of more experienced professionals. Short assignments and contract appointments are also symptoms of a malaise that limits learning experiences and career prospects.

Much of what project professional needs to learn, can only be acquired experientially 'on the job', and this needs to include genuine professional endeavour and adversity. It is through meeting personal challenge, engaging in dilemma and productive dialogue, experiencing the heat of disapproval and failure as well as the triumphs that a practitioner grows as a professional and as a leader.

And we are not only referring here to practitioners appointed as a project management professional. While a recognised project manager carries overall responsibility for the work, performance results from the combined efforts of all the project's players. They need their efforts and contributions as members of a project regime to be valued. Project management ability and temperaments are needed by them all. (It is worth remembering that APM in Britain stands for the Association for Project *Management* – not Project *Managers*.)

> *The development and maturity of a project practitioner is often interrupted when a career is put at risk in this still nascent discipline. Ken Livingstone, ex-Mayor of London, cites other threats to the development of able PM professionals.*

> *At 'Synergy 2011', a PMI UK Chapter event in London in November 2011, the ex-London mayor offered a downbeat assessment of UK*

project management talent, suggesting that if you want something doing properly, bring in outside help. He said that UK project chiefs had become 'stooges of bureaucracy' rather than challenging it. This had resulted in Barbara Cassini being brought in to run high-profile capital projects such as the London 2012 Olympics. 'We had to bring in an American woman to plan it and an Australian to build it', he said. Part of the tragedy of that is that Britain doesn't have a long-term conviction to invest in and develop projects to grow. Based on past experience, he said that Britain was capable of great things 'occasionally' but was failing to capture the lessons because the project innovators had either retired or passed away. This meant the profession having to learn it all over again (APM, 2011).

For too many aspiring professionals, project management fails to be attractive as a career choice and many businesses have difficulty in attracting sufficiently able aspirants to the role of a project management professional. There is widespread ignorance of the ethos of project management, its standards and practices. In some organisations the role has even become associated with being a 'fall-guy'. It is all too rare for professional jobseekers to be able to find a well-respected career path in project management – one that can be expected to attract opportunity, respect, professional standing and opportunity for genuine advancement.

Project management work can be particularly demanding of its players, relying as it does on the need to achieve demanding and ambitious goals that involve controversy and continual adaptation. Maybe it is for this reason that project management is sometimes referred to as 'extreme management'. Successful project players must be adept at compliance to a plan and schedule, while at the same time continually reviewing them with other players in the light of events and the learning opportunities that they provide. Project professionals must be both able and tenacious. They need to be encouraged and supported in building their role and reputation in this way.

In an interview with the Chartered Institute of Personnel and Development (CIPD) in October 2012, Gary Hamel, Professor of Strategic Management at London Business School, said:

Management was (originally) invented to turn human beings into semi-programmable robots. At the start of the industrial revolution, you needed people who could literally serve the machines. We took free-spirited, strong-willed people and turned them into forelock-tugging, biddable resources. Today, there are still plenty of occasions when we need people to do the same thing one hundred times in a row, very precisely; but we also need those same people to be lying awake at night thinking about the value of products or how to reinvent a production line.

The same person who is four or five rungs down at a big global retailer, just a cog in a machine, may be writing a blog at the weekend, redesigning their garden or creating beautiful photographs. The companies that win will be those who get a lot more than mere obedience or diligence from their people.

Hamel describes here a pattern of work that is implicit to project management. It has a distinct need for 'free-spirited and strong-willed people', as Hamel describes them. An ambitious agenda is needed for those who choose to associate with this professional endeavour.

In the professional institutions, certification of project management professionals, primary attention is given to the acquisition of knowledge and competencies. While vital, the dominance of these elements over other abilities and personal qualities have in the past served to mask the need for promoting the 'complete' ability of players – especially in the development of their own behaviour and their understanding of organisational behaviour. Yet these are critical and pervasive matters. The project management community needs to devise and promote a more complete and meaningful professional development path for resourcing, strengthening and enlarging an occupation that is vital to private, public and not-for-profit enterprise and the success of their organisations. This principle must also embrace the development of other professionals working from other functions who are also relied upon as project players.

Some practitioners appear to presume that to be managing a project is to be managing a process (see Chapter 4). This is a mistake as it presumes a universally applicable set of prescription for managing a project, for capturing ideas for improvement and coping with the choices between alternative courses of action.

When a fresh idea occurs to a player, some recognition is important to sustain their confidence and commitment. Leaders, in this way, need to show their regard for ingenuity, scrutiny and argument. Otherwise a valuable professional aspirant and maybe talent will be at risk of being overlooked –

prejudicing a player's personal and professional connection with their project regime, its vitality and that of the enterprise.

This book offers a fresh appreciation of how projects achieve and deliver satisfaction to customers, users and other stakeholders – and to do so reliably. Perhaps surprisingly, many of the approaches and methods described are drawn from past and present practice; albeit from exceptionally performing project regimes.

Project Players: The 'Venture Capital'

As a project develops, its uncertainties and their significance often seem to become increasingly certain. No matter how much we plan, what will then transpire, what will be learned and how this will affect later decisions cannot be known at the time. Whilst a business process might be assured with proven procedures, such routines are rarely the way of a project management endeavour. The nature of a project's purpose, its working arrangements and the uncertainties of the venture, are always unique. Progress can be expected only to be understood fully by the players themselves. The challenge of managing a project is one of continual planning and of resolving a series of situations and issues. The task is not one of conducting a prearranged process. If that is the experience, then it is not a project.

THE NEED FOR A COMPLETE AND COHERENT UNDERSTANDING

Many project management endeavours emerge as a triumph; but for others, factors that are sometimes beyond the control of the project manager and project sponsor can bring difficulties and failure. In many cases such disappointments can be attributed to shortcomings of management or leadership, or the project could well be using obsolescent practices. The players may be unaware of project management capability practiced in other places, signalling the need for the project management community to be more closely connected. To raise the capability and standing of project management, a more complete and coherent appreciation of the discipline needs to be widely appreciated and respected as an asset.

Projects vary immensely in the range and extent of the challenges that they present. The level of venture required varies accordingly (see Figure 1.1). At one end a predictable exercise can provide a practical response to well-known and thoroughly understood requirements and circumstances, and can be labelled

'Low Venture'. The project's purpose and stakeholder's expectations endure and the methods needed to achieve successful execution are generally reliable, defining what needs to be done, when and how.

At the other end of the scale however a project is fundamentally different. The circumstances and variables are more demanding to the extent that they become 'High Venture'. What has to be achieved and how are to an extent unpredictable and sometimes unknowable until the project is under way. The challenges include ambiguity, controversy, complexity and greater risk. Adaptability becomes increasingly important and the usefulness of any prescription falls away. The project regime's perspective is driven more by what is learned from issues as they emerge and from fresh insights than from any pre-packaged remedy. The challenges become predominantly human and organisational.

Throughout the world, economic and civic progress is now showing increasing dependence on High Venture projects and programmes. Their success demands a greater level of venture from the stakeholders. Delivery relies more on players' social engagement and collaboration than on standard or prescribed routines. In today's enterprise, a project's 'Venture Capital' has to be sufficiently capable and mature; with able players purposefully and professionally engaged.

PROPELLING A PROJECT ORGANISATION BY ITS VENTURE CAPITAL

In this environment, stakeholders have to draw heavily on their intuitive, social and organisational ability as well as on methodological and technical expertise. The project players are engaged in the most demanding of all tasks – tasks on which society's security and wealth generation increasingly depend. Resolve, quality of thinking, dialogue and organisational agility, collectively punch with more weight than any standard method can. Successful adaptation to the ongoing needs of a project must be orchestrated by all project players using a deliberate and venturesome approach.

CASE STUDY: A FAILURE OF VENTURESOME BEHAVIOUR

On 28 January 1986 the space shuttle *Challenger* tragically exploded shortly after lift-off (see Chapter 7). The official enquiry attributed the disaster to a fundamental organisational failure to properly examine and to act upon the risks attached to their decisions.

This is a stark example of how a lack of venturesome behaviour can bring difficulty, delay and ultimately disaster. Common human frailties include an unwillingness to listen, an absence of personal recognition, casual oversights, an absence of courage and courtesy, the perils of pride, a lack of grace and the side-lining of people showing reluctance to 'know their place'. By cultivating an environment where a venturesome attitude is embraced, these pitfalls can be avoided or overcome.

In project management this resolve manifests itself in a number of ways; observable as ambition, fear of failure, tenacity, collective intention, determination, professionalism, obstinacy, face and pride.

Professional Pointers

- It's no use saying 'We are doing our best'. You have got to succeed in doing what is necessary.

- Communities of practice.

- Venturesome behaviour.

- The risks of appointing inexperienced people to manage large and complex project ventures.

- Factors governing the fortunes of a project professional's career can run independently of their own choices and actions.

- The project team – an abiding myth.

- We must equip ourselves to be emotionally robust and avoid becoming a victim of the moment.

- Never lose the mask of relaxed brilliance.

- Britain doesn't have a long-term conviction to invest and develop projects to grow.

- The increasing dependence on high venture projects and programmes.

References

APM (2011), *Project Magazine*, Autumn.

Berg, S. (2012). Project megalomania: How the new Berlin Airport project fell apart. *Der Spiegel*, 19 November.

Cockburn, A. (2006). *Shu Ha Ri*. Available at: http://alistair.cockburn.us/Shu+Ha+Ri [accessed 7 May 2014].

Hillson, D. and Murray-Webster, R. (2005). *Understanding and Managing Risk Attitude*. Aldershot: Gower.

Katzenbach, J.R. and Smith, D.K. (1993). *The Wisdom of Teams: Creating the High-Performance Organization*. Boston, MA: Harvard Business School Press.

Levy, S. (2006). *The Perfect Thing: How the iPod Shuffles Commerce, Culture, and Coolness*. London: Random House.

Merrrow, E.W. (2011). *Industrial Megaprojects: Concepts, Strategies, and Practices for Success*. Hoboken, NJ: Wiley.

NAO (2013). *The Major Projects Report 2012*. London: National Audit Office.

Pralahad, C.K. and Hamel, G.P. (1990). The core competence of the corporation. *Harvard Business Review*, 68(3): 79–91.

Prince, L. (2008). Eating the menu rather than the dinner: Tao and leadership. *Leadership*, 1(1): 105–26.

Saint-Onge, H. and Wallace, D. (2003). *Leveraging Communities of Practice for Strategic Advantage*. Boston, MA: Butterworth-Heinemann.

Schön, D. (1983). *The Reflective Practitioner: How Professionals Think in Action*. New York: Basic Books.

Seery, M.D. (2010). Whatever does not kill us: Cumulative lifetime adversity, vulnerability, and resilience. *Journal of Personality and Social Psychology*, 99(6): 1025–41.

Vaughan, D. (1996). *The Challenger Launch Decision*. Chicago, IL: University of Chicago Press.

Wagner, R. (2006). *The Elements of Great Managing*. New York: Gallup.

Wenger, E. (1998). *Communities of Practice: Learning, Meaning, and Identity*. Cambridge: Cambridge University Press.

Chapter 3
A Project's Strength

From Player's Leadership, Ensuring Astute Navigation and Progress

---

With players examining issues before showing ways to progress with resolve, ingenuity, strategic thinking, professionalism, good judgment and teamwork.

Refer to the Nine Crucial Capabilities

Introduction

The uncertainty, novelty, adaptation, rigour, close collaboration and other pioneering features of project management help to distinguish it as a discrete and separate management discipline. The crucial behaviours of players rely upon their resolve, professionalism, dialogue, imagination and the dedication and strength of a project's sponsors.

Leaders: those formally appointed and others simply responding to emergent issues, need to address concerns and opportunities with passion and rigour to ensure and enhance the project's pace of progress. The need for thoughtful and responsible leadership in any group is central and must never be regarded as an added extra. That would be to mis-understand the nature and ethos of the discipline. An understanding of the strength of a project regime can be observed from the autonomy that is evident; as this is permitted by the stakeholders and the way that this is sustained.

Resolute Leadership

We have to be very clear about our expectations of a regime's leadership: the capacity of all its players to contribute to 'showing the way forward'. We rely on leaders to avoid waste, mistakes and error, while also depending on them to exploit opportunity. A project carries risks that will either limit or strengthen the venture, and these need to be contained to the unavoidable. Progress and distinction will be gained or lost, usually depending on the players' qualities of diligence – a feature of leadership.

We recognise the work of leaders when we see players energised and empowered to pursue and to do what matters: acting with reason, risk awareness, judgement, discretion and tenacity. In project work adaptation is continual, making leadership crucial to success.

Project decisions must be astute and often subject to the will of the regime: skilfully applied and, so far as can be foreseen, robust to upcoming events. As for any organisation, they are strengthened by having a robust long-term perspective and ambitions. Exercising leadership is an obligation on all players, with the greatest obligation to the more experienced and senior.

By way of illustration, the following accounts reveal what can be called 'resolute leadership'. Here, players at the apex of their enterprise have championed an innovative endeavour, expressing a resolute leadership that mobilised collective intention and a preparedness to consent to risk. In their role as a project manager, they can be recognised to assess opportunity and its benefits, shape and scope the project, set the objectives, secure support, plan and manage its execution and delivery.

The projects described here, and for which these executives have been responsible, help show the importance of resolute leadership as a feature of project management.

LEE KUN-HEE, CHAIRMAN OF SAMSUNG GROUP

Today Samsung's revenues are 39 times what they were in 1987 when Lee Kun-hee was appointed chairman upon the death of his father, Lee Byung-chull. He wrote that a successful company needs a 'heightened sense of crisis', so that it always looks ahead even when it is doing well and is thereby able to respond to challenges and change. A Japanese journalist reported 'the involuntary devotion of its workers', such has been the regard for the Lee family and the devotion of employees to their enterprise (Michell, 2010).

A community ethos has driven Samsung Electronics to be one of the world's largest technology firms – it sells more televisions, smartphones and memory chips than any other. Semiconductors and mobile phones are Samsung's flagship products today, but it went through significant difficulties in its early days. Lee took the decision to invest heavily in the mobile phone business, but in 1993 – and when they did not show the early success anticipated – he ordered the incineration of defective mobile phones worth billions, largely as a signal of collective intention. He was, as other Korean businessmen, an exponent of the principle of 'double or quits' in which unstinting up-front investment expects and wins early market entry and the margin and advantage that this brings. A year after this defining event, the domestic market share jumped to 19 per cent and it has continuously grown to become the global top seller today.

In comparison with its competitors, Samsung has always placed strong emphasis on refining recruitment, staff development and employee commitment to the company. In 2004, with other measures to heighten performance, Lee outlined the factors and qualities that would help Samsung reach its goals. It was known as '7 DNA'. They were:

1.   Dream, vision and goal.

2.   Insight and good sense.

3.   Trust and credibility.

4.   Creativity and challenge.

5.   Technology and information.

6.   Speed and velocity.

7.   Change and innovation.

SIR RICHARD BRANSON

Branson has been tagged as a 'transformational leader'. He claims that the Virgin Group that he founded is an organisation that is bottom-heavy rather than strangled by top-level management. Branson entered the business world while still at school, and then steadily built up his enterprise by retaining personal ownership of the Virgin brand and many of its businesses. Across its companies, Virgin employs approximately 50,000 people in 34 countries, and global branded revenues in 2011 were around £13 billion ($21 billion). The commercial arrangement of companies licensed to use the brand is, however, varied and complex. Quoting from the virgin website:

> The Virgin Group of companies is part of one big family rather than a hierarchy. They are empowered to run their own affairs, yet the companies actively help one another and solutions to problems are often sourced from within the Group. In a sense they form a commonwealth, with shared ideas, values, interest and goals. Virgin believes in making a difference. 'We stand for value for money, quality, innovation, fun and a sense of competitive challenge'. We strive to achieve this by empowering our employees to continually deliver an unbeatable customer experience.

Business decisions in Virgin's businesses carrying the brand appear to be devolved locally and the proponents are notably trusting. As a leader, Branson looks to manage delegation as exercising a commercial relationship. Sometimes his writing suggests also that this engagement is also conducted in a way that relies on strong personal relationships (Branson, 2011).

SIR RALPH ROBINS

Sir Ralph is the unsung hero of Rolls-Royce in Britain. He was chairman up to his retirement in 2003 after 43 years with the company and then the longest-serving employee.

He was cited by James Naughty on BBC Radio 4 in his series on the New Elizabethans in April 2012. Sir Ralph is attributed with successfully defending a major UK business from take-over from a US or Japanese company – the way in which many UK firms in the post-war period were bought out. He led successful bids for strategic sales at a critical time, including a £1 billion order for Trent jet engines from American Airlines. He was seen as a shrewd deal-maker.

Robins was very critical of British banks' short-termism in their refusal to value Rolls-Royce properly, their insistence on quick returns and their failure to recognise the company's need for long-term investment. There is some doubt whether Rolls-Royce as an independent firm would have survived without Robins' leadership in this period.

Sir John Rose, ex-CEO and fellow board member who retired in 2010, described the business's survival – commercially, financially and as an organisation in Robins' time – as a 'close-run thing' and referred to his 'balls of steel'.

STEVE JOBS

Like the other resolute leaders described here, Steve Jobs distinguished himself with a leadership style that emerged from his own personal view of himself and the world. He was always curious, imaginative and venturesome, and this was constantly evident in his style of leadership. In 1985 Apple Inc. reached a low ebb in its fortunes, and Jobs was effectively dismissed. On his return 11 years later, his resolve to build the business attained new heights into what very quickly became the second largest information technology business in the world.

His dominant style in leading market and product development included what came to be known as the 'Reality Distortion Field' (see Chapter 1) in which he would insist on the incorporation of features that many considered to be impossible. Despite others' scepticism, many were in fact realised and incorporated into world-beating products.

There is evidently no universal platform for building resolute leadership. Luck must play a part – but there must be passion, insight and fine judgement in determining the most reliable routes to a goal.

BP ANDREW FIELD (SEE CHAPTER 1) AND ROCKY FLATS CLEAN-UP (SEE CHAPTER 9)

These projects also demonstrate Resolute Leadership deployed in depth and throughout the venture. In both cases, the regime became conducive to the devolution of leadership and innovation at all levels of the organisation: widening the bandwidth of argument and dialogue to achieve outstanding results from working collaboratively, thoroughly, profitably and devoid of unnecessary delay.

Causes of Project Failure

A mass of research has sought to identify and explain the causes of project difficulty and failure. Projects with a faulted history are not difficult to find, and many surveys to explain this have been published over the last 15 years. These include work by PMI, the British Computer Society, the National Audit Office, the Standish Organisation and the US Department of Defense. They typically list a summary of the areas of project management where it is concluded that greater care and attention had been required. These lists of what are often called 'lessons learned' differ substantially in their contents and conclusion, but they all refer to the importance of the behaviour of players and their organisation.

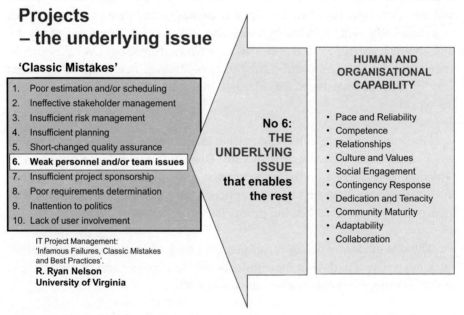

Figure 3.1   Classic Mistakes
Source: 2012 © EngagementWorks Ltd.

In Figure 3.1 the list of 'classic mistakes' is reproduced from a paper by R. Ryan Nelson (2007). Item 6 of these, 'Weak personnel and/or team issues', is a reference to the behaviours of players and their project regime. It suggests that Item 6 amounts to the underlying issue, or even the root cause of all the classic mistakes. This capability can be recognised to make a substantial contribution towards resolving the other nine, implying that it is a primary root cause of failure.

Surveys of failure strongly outnumber reports that seek to understand reasons for success. We know that failure can be characterised by 'failure modes' that trace common patterns of error, mistakes and difficulty; but any claim that the knowledge and ability needed to ensure success can be best acquired from an understanding of failure, rests on a weak argument. To learn retrospectively this way, expecting to progress the practices of project management is surely a mistake.

Such assumptions about the value of lessons learned might explain the frustration experienced by institutions, leaders and commentators when in pursuit of measures to achieve performance improvement. Any attempt to maximise the success of a project must surely seek novel thinking and practices, relying on new ideas and innovation more than on retrospective studies of failures and the weaknesses that are claimed to have caused them.

The players' enterprise is an important ingredient of a successful project, but it is an aspect of project management that continues to be under-stated. It is not a condition that is easily definable; but reports of economic growth by businesses based in the Far East quickly reveal that their enduring sense of enterprise is a major factor and this is explicitly claimed by its exponents.

And for projects characterised by significant complexity and uncertainty, we should be suspicious of any idea that there could be 'silver bullets' that will herald success. Once the 'hygiene factors' (an analogous reference here to Henry Herzberg's theory of motivation) are secured as a base-line capability, the factors that triumph over project adversity are those that are particular to a project regime. Distinctive, competitive and innovative project management is situation-specific rather than being attributable to compliance with declared professional standards or a recognised methodology.

Improvements to any management endeavour depend on the discovery and application of the most progressive thinking and ingenuity, emerging from human and organisational behaviour. People's behaviour, whether working singly or in groups, maps the root causes of both difficulty and success (or 'risk'). Behaviours include creativity, carelessness, persistence, leadership, naivety, oversight, denial, dispute, collaboration, social interaction, obfuscation, ambition, engagement, discipline, willingness, collaboration, political adroitness, ignorance and courage. All are derived from the unique qualities of people and their organisation.

To find a more coherent rationale for managing projects, readers may find that the principles and approaches that can be found in this book will offer some help. Comprehensive and insightful principles and practices addressing themselves to human behaviour are needed to complement methodology and other systematic schemas now promoted and deployed by project practitioners as the universal formula for this discipline.

Ideas are offered here to assist readers to devise and deploy stronger plans for realising their performance and reliability goals. A project calls upon its players to be both systematic and venturesome. Leadership is a pervasive and progressive source of a regime's strength and vitality needed for managing its pace of progress (see Chapter 6). A project under development is an unpredictable place, and leadership cannot be regarded as 'the icing on the cake'. In project management in particular, leadership, a crucial ingredient of adaptation, is the key driver. The reader will find references to 'Venture Capital' in Chapter 2.

Contrasting Project Work with Line-of-Business Work

Many, if not most project regimes exist to serve line-of-business organisations and their different working arrangements can lead to difficulties. The uncertainty, risks and complexity that characterise project management can be disconcerting to executives unfamiliar with a pioneering agenda. This is illustrated by business executives who, despite their dependence on the success of projects, sometimes have no more than a fleeting knowledge of the function and how it can be expected to progress.

Some, who we can refer to as 'host executives', often fail to connect with the unpredictability and apparent disorder that accompanies a project management endeavour. They can be heard to say, 'They are all professionals in their own right: they collect information, they evaluate it and then use it to solve problems just like the rest of us'. Project management professionals need to be asking themselves, more than sometimes they do, whether they value and champion the exacting situations that they routinely encounter and endure and that are implicit to their trade.

So, how well is the difference between working on a business process (e.g. sales, cost accounting, marketing, production etc.) and managing a project generally understood? Of course there are some businesses that are entirely devoted to managing projects (examples include some engineering construction businesses), where everyone in some way is deployed as a project player. But in many projects also, project players are seconded from other functions, and it is important that they are able to adjust to the working practices of project management. An academic in project management, when pressed to answer the question 'What distinguishes project management from other management work?', is reputed to have answered, 'They manage a life-cycle'. We need to ask ourselves whether this provides us with a sufficient understanding for accommodating the crucial differences.

When a project regime is embedded within a business organisation, one that is essentially unfamiliar with project management, the host, as sponsor, is often seen to place undue limitations on the discretion that is allowed. The traditions and preferences of the host – as these are expressed in their own familiar processes and culture, relationships and patterns of accountability – can often operate very differently to the conduct found in a project management function.

A capable project regime requires a professional freedom of action; to be able to respond to events. If it is not capable of acquiring this then measures need to be taken that makes it so. Delegation of authority to a project regime by its host organisation often needs continual and careful attention.

Stanley Deetz, Professor at the University of Colorado in Boulder, in his 2003 Becker lecture said:

> In today's world, unless you have exceptionally low labour costs, competitive advantage comes from high creativity, highly committed employees and the ability to customize products. All require a very involved and participating workforce. Creativity requires us to allow differences to make a difference. Most high-end companies know that they are more dependent on the social and intellectual capital possessed by employees than on financial investment.

Deetz's vision of the qualities required of organisations today offers a valuable pointer to the way in which project professionals must assert their functional and professional authority if they are to make the contribution that their customers and circumstances demand.

For a project regime to be sufficiently responsive to the demands for performance improvement and innovation, players as professionals and leaders in workgroups must be responsive and adaptable. Otherwise progress will be slow, opportunities lost and energy will be quickly spent. It is the experience of players, their resolve, knowledge and capacity for engagement, collaboration and pace that enable progress.

A project regime operates through the sensing, thinking and the social engagement of its players, and this relies on purposeful and dedicated dialogue. Without this we cannot expect the generation and distillation of creativity and the rigour that is needed to make progress. Social engagement must inspire and sustain the reasoning necessary for acquiring collective intention and to navigate a progressive course. Dialogue is also necessary to dislodge the inhibitions that can beset command structures.

Could it be that all work is steadily becoming projectised? The distinction between project working and line-of-business working is in many instances now being eroded – with businesses that are regularly changing their products, materials, supply chains, distribution channels, market positioning and the technologies on which they depend. The patterns of work that sustain enterprise in all sectors also change with these changing goals. So prowess in the capability to manage projects now and in the future will meet an increasingly universal and growing need.

Showing the Way through Leadership

As Robert Majure, senior programme manager of the aerospace core programme, Honeywell Aerospace, stated:

> For good project management, you … need personality, power and persona. It takes a lot of leadership skills to drive a complex project through a complex organisation. Tools alone can't make that happen (Economist Intelligence Unit, 2009).

Karlin Sloan, a leading executive coach, in her book *Smarter, Better, Faster*, reminds us that 'things are often not what they seem to be'. She says:

> Traditional (or should I call it 'twentieth century'?) business thinking holds that being smarter means gathering knowledge, learning more and more and becoming a certified expert. It used to be that being a smart leader meant that you simply knew more than anyone else.
>
> But now, information is managed in entirely different ways. Information, thanks in large part to the internet, is accessible to all. So, in the twenty

first century, being smart often means knowing how to manage and distribute information; not necessarily knowing the information itself. The idea that the leader is the authority on all things no longer holds.

So if information itself does not make a leader smarter, then what does? Herein lays the paradox. Today it is the ability to ask powerful questions that makes a leader smarter. It is a tolerance of ambiguity and to see the big picture – to see the impact of decision-making on a complex system.

Today's leaders must know how to get the information that they seek, how to inspire others to actions from that information and how to surround themselves with the intellectual capital that extends far beyond their own. To be smarter we need to stop being the expert and start asking more questions (Sloane, 2006: ix).

'Leading', while universally regarded for its value, resists a clear and simple description, calling as it does upon people's reason, courage, experience, social interaction, discipline and resolve. Project management professionals have to take responsibility for their project's direction of travel and the choices that they make. They must do this in their engagement with the others: making sense of situations, reviewing earlier decisions and sense stakeholder's interests with authenticity.

The readiness of all players to respond and act in this way lies at the heart of professional ability and a successful project undertaking. Projects that bring us value are the result of the efforts of functional specialists and of competent and mature professional players acting their part in a community of commitments: being venturesome, accepting the management of risks and acting purposefully, in concert with others.

Mike Myatt, author of *Leadership Matters: The CEO Survival Manual* (2008), talks about what is perhaps the most misunderstood aspect of great leadership:

A leader simply operates at their best when they understand their ability to influence is much more fruitful than their ability to control. Here's the thing – the purpose of leadership is not to shine the spotlight on yourself, but to unlock the potential of others so they can in turn, shine the spotlight on countless more. Control is about power – not leadership. Surrender allows a leader to get out of their own way and focus on adding value to those whom they serve (Myatt, 2012).

The exercise of power is a crucial element of managing any organisation. It must be moderated by the need to draw upon the wit, wisdom and energy available from all its players.

Binary Leadership

We can recognise 'leading' as manifested in two quite separate but interrelated ways. In the first, 'Natural Leadership' (Blank, 1995) it is about attending to the immediate needs of people and groups and their behaviour; informing their understanding, connections, learning, engagement, choices and co-operation, and in doing so relying on the capacity for reasoning and natural law.[1] In the second, what we might call 'Purposeful Leadership', it is to serve and enable the purpose, direction and pace of progress of an enterprise as promoted through its principles and goals. It is to ensure that followers exercise responsibilities as determined by the senior managers.

The purpose of leadership is a popular subject in many commentaries on project management and there is a preoccupation with behaviour. There is, however, another and more rational and compelling case for leadership – namely it is the function that has to be resorted to in decision-making when an objective analysis of facts has itself been found to be unsatisfactory or insufficient. Leadership then has the obligation to step in and offer method or direction – using its judgement, reasoning, lateral thinking and a consideration of alternative actions.

Only when social capital is actively cultivated and deployed can human and organisational capability be appreciated for its value as an asset. Claims of 'people being our most valuable asset' often don't hold true in organisations that boast the mantra when the habits of social engagement and collaboration are underdeveloped. The qualities of the players' ability to work in groups, their resolve, critical thinking, communication, clear-headedness and social interaction, can only be realised when the project regime is fully engaged, inspired and stretched towards its limits. Projects absolutely depend on this dynamic capability as the engine of their success. The extent of the players'

---

1   According to natural law theory, which holds that morality is a function of human nature and reason can discover valid moral principles by looking at the nature of humanity in society, the content of positive law cannot be known without some reference to natural law. Used in this way, natural law can be invoked to criticise decisions about the statutes, but less so to criticise the law itself. Some use natural law synonymously with natural justice or natural right (Wikipedia).

resolve, dialogue and mobilisation represents a project regime's venture capital (see Chapter 2). This is always hard-won and, for project work, the need is relentless and easily stood down.

Professional Pointers

- The capacity of all players to 'show the way'.

- Like any organisation, they are strengthened by having a robust long-term perspective and ambitions.

- A successful company needs a 'heightened the sense of crisis'.

- They are empowered to run their own affairs.

- A project calls upon its players to be both systematic and venturesome.

- Leadership cannot be regarded as 'the icing on the cake'. It is the key driver.

- The host is often seen to place undue limitations on the discretion of the project regime.

- Social engagement must inspire and sustain the reasoning necessary for acquiring collective intention.

- Diversity trumps ability.

- To be smarter, we need to stop being the expert and start asking more questions.

- Control is about power – not leadership.

References

Blank, W. (1995). *The 9 Natural Laws of Leadership*. New York: American Management Association (AMACOM).

Branson, R. (2011). *Screw Business as Usual*. London: Virgin.

Economist Intelligence Unit (2009). *Closing the Gap: The Link between Project Management Excellence and Long-Term Success*. A report sponsored by Oracle. Available at: http://www.projectmanagement.ie/userfiles/files/Economist_Intelligence_Unit_PM_Excellence.pdf.

Michell, T. (2010). *Samsung Electronics and the Struggle for Leadership of the Electronics Industry*. Singapore: Wiley.

Myatt, M. (2008). *Leadership Matters: The CEO Survival Manual: What it Takes to Reach the C-Suite, and Stay There*. Denver, CO: Outskirts Press.

Myatt, M. (2012). The most misunderstood aspect of great leadership. *Forbes*, 26 December. Available at: http://www.forbes.com/sites/mikemyatt/2012/12/26/the-most-misunderstood-aspect-of-great-leadership [accessed 28 December 2012].

Nelson, R.R. (2007). IT project management: Infamous failures, classic mistakes and best practices. *MIS Quarterly Executive*, 6(2): 67–79.

Page, S.E. (2007). *The Difference: How the Power of Diversity Creates Better Groups, Firms, Schools, and Societies*. Princeton, NJ: Princeton University Press.

Prince, L. (2008). Eating the menu rather than the dinner: The Tao of leadership. *Leadership*, 1(1): 105–26.

Sloan, K. (2006). *Smarter, Better, Faster: Strategies for Effective, Enduring, and Fulfilled Leadership*. San Francisco, CA: Jossey-Bass.

PART II
Conducting the Work

Chapter 4

A Project's Connections

Enabling Players to Exploit Possibilities and Bring Synergy

> Building the capacity to maximise the pace of progress. Enriching the players' network, enabling engagement, scrutiny, resolve and resilience.
>
> *Refer to the Nine Crucial Capabilities*

Introduction

A principal goal of any project regime must be to capture and deploy the ideas, energy and perspectives of participants committed to the venture. The regime is always an important source of risks that will either threaten or enhance progress. To accommodate these risks and to maximise the pace of progress, the regime relies on connections across a network of participants or players. Drawing on the analogy of the human brain, each cell has an important function – but only when they connect can they play their part.

Connections serve to link and combine ideas, energy and perspectives that then enable goals and plans to be shaped and developed. A project regime can only progress with purposeful and venturesome dialogue conducted through a network of connections. All this is to enable robust and progressive project execution and delivery.

Project work can be the most demanding of all human endeavours and to succeed the conduct of players need in this way to be methodical, concerted and single-minded. For any regime seeking a strong pace of progress, 'taking the lead' characterises the conduct of every group with players also performing effectively as individual contributors.

This chapter presents project management activity depending on the leadership and social engagement of every player. A feeble lament exhorting people to 'improve communication around here' is always entirely inadequate. Adaptation is critical to maximising a project's pace of progress with responsibilities devolved to groups across the regime. The project manager bears overall responsibility and needs to support and promote the autonomy of work groups while assuring that the necessary connections within the regime are sustained.

The Engagement Capability of groups (see later in this chapter) is needed to harness the abilities and interests of all players, is the foundation for collaboration. It is examined here in some detail and a means of measuring this capability is described. Connections depend on the quality of dialogue and the chapter explores ways to enrich this through conversation. A project's performance can be substantially improved in the presence of a project management community and a development framework is described to induct newcomers to build and sustain project community maturity (see page 105).

Players Working in Concert

Projects are often complex; with a purpose and plans that change. Tasks and their responsibilities have to adapt over a project's life-cycle; responding to changes to the requirement and from emergent issues arising from work in progress. The role of those who must ensure connections and the local discretion that they allow, is captured by a comment from 'David' speaking from the role of a senior manager in an organisation that has been purposely devolved to encourage local adaptation:

> My basic job I think is to help my team to buy into a different way of working: to be a provider of enablement. I provide people with contacts, intellectual context, the resources and delivery framework for their activity; a sounding board for ideas and a source of critical reflection through conversation. Indeed, sometimes the people who report to me 'lead' and I follow. I applaud this. (Awati, 2011)

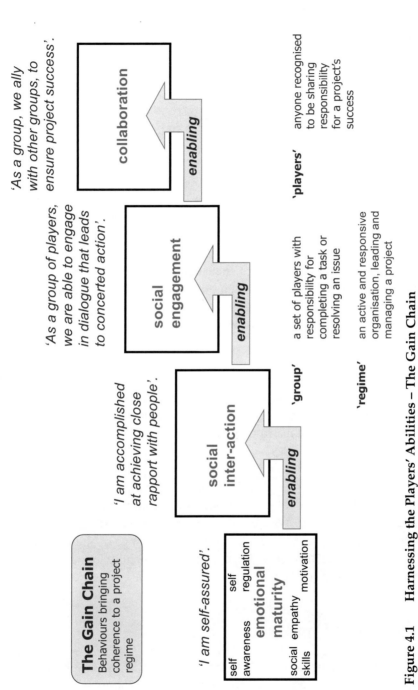

Figure 4.1   Harnessing the Players' Abilities – The Gain Chain

Source: 2012 © EngagementWorks Ltd.

As in an expedition, a project must progress through unfamiliar territory where, in contrast with the more regular procedures of a business process, routes to progress have first to be discovered and selected. Conduct can be complex and irregular, and a project regime must accommodate the disruption introduced by new and emergent requirements. These will demand the execution of new tasks and the adaptation of others already in train (see the 'Tacking Cycle' in Chapter 8). A project's progress is characterised by continual adaptation, responding to the discovery of opportunities and constraints.

Figure 4.1, on the previous page, offers a simple representation of how a regime's players can leverage its connections: progressing through successive stages and advancing along what is termed the 'Gain Chain'. The first stage depends on the player's emotional maturity, an essential foundation for competence and the ability on which other skills and behaviours depend. Emotional intelligence that underlies emotional maturity is a concept developed by Daniel Goleman in his book of that name (1995). Players equipped with the personal qualities derived from emotional maturity (Hillson and Murray-Webster, 2005) have acquired many of the foundations of self-awareness, self-regulation, social skills, empathy and motivation that serves useful social interaction.

Players then equipped with a capacity for social interaction can relate, converse and share their observations and ideas with other players. This way, a working group can expect to acquire the Engagement Capability needed to harness their combined skills, knowledge and interests, to then act in concert to achieve the group's objectives.

This will then prepare them for open, disciplined and venturesome dialogue; collaborating with other groups to maximise the project's pace of progress (see Chapter 6). We cannot expect to be harnessing everyone's full potential and all players have their own particular range of abilities and parts to play; but once socially engaged, the combined capability of working groups can then expect to address issues most productively.

Leveraging from Diversity

The argument developed by Scott E. Page in *The Difference* is summarised by his maxim 'diversity trumps ability' (Page, 2007). He argues how 'collective wisdom' (or the more familiar idea of 'the wisdom of crowds' by James Surowiecki), when properly harvested, is of greater value than the sum of its parts. Work groups, when able to learn from an aggregation of perspectives, consistently outperform like-minded experts when functioning individually. For this to happen, a regime has to be astute and open in its conversation, always venturesome, able to recognise hitherto unimagined constraints and to seize those occasions when rich and rigorous dialogue is required.

Engagement and Decision-Making

Any project regime will seek to align its goals with the interests of its stakeholders and players. But there are many interests at stake and all must somehow be embraced and reconciled where necessary. Customers and their users will have their preferences, suppliers their commercial interests, governments their policy and regulations, functions their preferred working practices and players their ambitions, careers and reputations to pursue and defend.

Acquiring and scrutinising the information needed to make decisions requires the players' dedicated resolve, dialogue and organisation. The original studies by EngagementWorks into the priorities and behaviour of project players showed that a majority of players' time is devoted to resolving these matters. This time is however, not always well spent, despite this being in the place where project management is conducted and transacted. Managing the pace of progress depends on social engagement applied with prompt and diligent attention to decision-making.

Politicians need their parliament, lawyers their chambers, armies their headquarters and academics their campus. Project practitioners, in seeking to advance their project, also need a forum in which to share professional matters and issues, reflect on them and to progress their endeavour. The places available to a regime for active dialogue and reflective conversation include offices, corridors, telephones, trains, planes, meeting rooms, conferences, email, tweeting or in shared meals. Players have to make opportunities to meet, address, examine and inform their choices. In project management, such opportunities can be elusive and professionals have to be proactive if they are to ensure that places for dialogue and argument are made to be available.

Some project groups in a regime will remain intact over long periods, but others will form and then disband more quickly. And it is difficult and sometimes impossible for the members of a group to share the time and the place that they need. Through their leadership, players need to secure opportunities for social engagement; ensuring that what has to be said is said and heard. Stand-ins, phone-ins and preparatory conversations may often be expedient, but face-to-face encounters can be crucial to the pace of progress and reliably. The role of a project player demands ingenuity, to remain aware of activities and their progress, to be involved in decision-making and to share responsibility as circumstances demand.

Dialogue and Its Diversity

Dialogue is both a form of connecting and a way of relating, to achieve clarity of understanding and shared commitment. It is a form of communication in which participants should expect to say or hear something otherwise never to be said or shared. It is a place from which players emerge with an enriched understanding of the issues and fresh options for ways to progress. Dialogue emphasises listening, learning, probing and uncovering what otherwise might be left unspoken. It is a pre-requisite for decision-making and if dialogue is reliant upon email, telephone and other social media, additional competences are required beyond those needed in a face-to-face situation.

Dialogue differs from other modes of social exchange, including mediation, negotiation, discussion and debate. In a debate, players seek to persuade others of their correctness and of the legitimacy of their position. Ideas are batted back and forth, exposing multiple perspectives. People seek to justify and defend their positions and to convince others of their correctness. Those with limited experience of debate can become defensive or reactive. Attitudes to others, the importance of the subject to someone and the perceived importance of issues will have their impact.

In dialogue, participants seek to discover, inform and learn rather than to overtly persuade. Improvement to understanding is its purpose. Candour cannot succeed without a receptive audience and players cannot be allowed to restrict their concerns to their own views and positions. They know that they are also obliged to comprehend and learn from the arguments advanced by other players. The participants need to focus on collective responsibilities, relationships social engagement and productive outcomes more than on winning or losing.

Dialogue has no predetermined agenda other than the regime's objectives. In project management, dialogue is vital to connect, engage and collaborate. The emphasis is not on resolving disputes, but on improving the way in which people relate to one another when there are different perspectives or interests to be reconciled. The aim is for the members of a group to think together: to promote appreciative inquiry (Cooperrider et al., 2008) and to stimulate conversation that is open minded; allowing important issues to be tabled, fully understood and resolved and the project progressed.

Exerting some control over dialogue by a manager who is exercising their positional authority will sometimes be necessary. However, if this approach is unwisely deployed it can raise the risk of a decision being reached from an insufficient understanding of the subject at hand and may lessen the commitment of those who are then to bear responsibility for its implementation. The quality of dialogue, relationships and the motivation of players are major factors in moderating these uncertainties.

Reaching for a Dialogue beyond Differences

People sometimes lack the willingness to converse on a subject that they know to be important and an impasse can then disrupt progress. This can happen when players address an issue arising from different interpretations of the same facts or from events that may not have been fully understood. Apparently irreconcilable differences in preferences and values can encourage players to hold on to their position while demeaning the views of their adversaries. Dialogue will in some cases require an intervention that will break a spell of silence – these often arising from political factors that have been allowed to disrupt the dialogue.

Parties often fail to pose questions or to sense intentions by failing to listen to what others are seeking to convey. While someone is talking, others are not properly listening as they allow their own mind to restrict itself to what they wish themselves to express. Communication can be inhibited by competition, prejudice and fear and so the ways of relating can become restricted. There can be heartfelt feelings and remarks that dwell on the apparent moral or logical flaws recognised in the positions expressed by others and this can easily inhibit progress.

Players often seek to rely on rhetoric and become defensive in the face of evidence that their own proposition might be unacceptable. Motives can appear to be questionable. Stereotyping can also lead to a polarisation of positions. Conversation can become threatening, characterised by personal attack and interruption. Even when players are secretly undecided about an issue; they might fail to voice their reservations.

An inexperienced player will sometimes fear that if they do not hold on to a weakening position, they will look lame or be censured by their colleagues. Repeated statements expressing entrenched positions can close people off from listening, comprehending ideas and openly questioning them. Parties might simply argue more loudly and refuse to be receptive to the views of others. Polarisation poses significant barriers to engagement and collaboration, making problem-solving difficult. So much depends upon the player's rigour, capacity to formulate ideas and argue their case, and on those players who are able to perform well as leaders, to moderate these encounters and the attitudes of players.

Players sometimes need to find fresh ways of relating to one another. Maybe before they sit down to address the main event, players anticipating conflicting positions might first engage in a preliminary conversation where these matters can be aired informally and clarified before the formalities. In a serious dialogue, a group is more likely to be able to handle surprises than shocks and courtesy, if genuine, can win people over – if only as a way of recruiting protagonists into an alliance relationship as an investment in a project's future.

Collective Intention

Every project depends on its Collective Intention (see Chapter 6). It serves to focus on a regime's purpose and once established provides the routes available to adaptation.

Let us look at an example. In the mid-1950s a business now known as Toyota had just one factory and was largely unknown, even in Japan. At that time its founders declared their intention to become the world's most successful manufacturer of motor cars (Liker, 2004). They then set about forming the strategies, plans, resources, methods and skills that they needed to realise their ambition.

Their conviction led to the re-invention of motor car manufacturing and eventually to becoming a global 'number one'. In today's competitive and fast-developing world it becomes increasingly clear that an enterprise depends more than ever on its resolve and sometimes a stubbornness, to realise its potential. 'Business as usual' has become obsolescent, overtaken by continuous improvement, short product life-cycles and repeated organisational makeovers.

More complex projects require more venturesome behaviour. For instance, for the civil engineer the development of a large tidal power generation facility will present more unknowns than are likely to be encountered in building a standard multi-storey car park.

When managing a project we are not only depending on the quality and strength of individuals' intentions, but also the more challenging ambition to mobilising multiple players to sign on to what are always unique and unproven collective intentions. Multiple parties must, through their resolve, dialogue and organisation, strive to fashion, agree and formulate some form of alliance. The quality of a group's collective intention has proved through history to be crucial as a performance multiplier.

Behaviour

Behaviour is what people do, and it originates from their perceptions and thinking. Using the term can feel awkward when describing the conduct of professionals. We are very accustomed to hear a mother call out 'behave!' to her mischievous children, and for many of us the memory of this can be a distraction. However, it remains as the only word to refer to what people do, so we stick with it here.

The word has in recent years come to be used widely in referring to any action of a person or a group. This book addresses the behaviour of project players as they go about managing a project. More specifically, it refers to project players sensing, thinking, acting, relating, and engaging with one another before making choices. 'Behaviour' is used here interchangeably with 'conduct'.

BEHAVIOUR: A WORTHY PARTNER TO METHODOLOGY

Harry referred to himself a project manager when he presented his project plan. He announced that this was developed using standard templates but he looked puzzled when asked how well his plan showed what he intended to achieve and how it recognised uncertainties. 'Yes of course', he said. 'I have followed the project management processes'. This response did not answer the question and implied some confusion on Harry's part.

Had he considered more than one scenario and explored the uncertainties? Had he discussed the plan with possible stakeholders and examined the scope, shape, risks and assumptions, to learn about their own ideas and views and to win their support? Did they accept the anticipated costs, timescales and contingencies? Were options shared with stakeholders and had the foundations of a project management community been laid? How well did stakeholders understand what was possible to understand at this stage? Had they 'signed up' to the venture?

Harry saw the task to be essentially one of complying with a standardised process that had been prescribed. For a low venture and relatively predictable project, such a prescriptive approach can be sufficient. But for a high venture and high risk project (the subject of this book), such behaviour would be equivalent to a pilot flying in poor visibility across unfamiliar territory without navigational aids. They may well have had clear intentions as to where they were headed, but they were ill-prepared for the unexpected.

Someone once described managing a project as 'simple but not easy' and it was Peter Drucker, the management writer, who made the distinction between 'doing the right things' and 'doing things right' (see Figure 5.1). In complying with a methodology, Harry was 'doing the right things'. But we have to ask whether he was also being sufficiently diligent to 'do things right'. In particular, was he persistently determined to complete the project successfully or was he more inclined simply to follow a prescribed process? A full commitment to the management of a project and its uncertainties, extends the agenda for reasoning what then has to be done – to 'do things right'.

For a professional this is routine: enquiring, questioning, engaging, exploring, and considering matters and issues in preparing for making a decision. Through the regime's connections, professional players will ensure that their engagement prepares them to secure the necessary collaboration.

In contrast with the story of Harry, an account follows of a project manager in a third world country who habitually reaches for ways to enhance a regime's connections. Bikas was one of six project managers implementing a programme to assist the development of village communities in the Kathmandu Valley in Nepal. The mission was to deploy projects to raise the quality of healthcare, education, nutrition and enterprise by training and supporting local people to make measurable improvements. Each project manager had a motorbike and every day they would follow the same routine; setting off early in the morning from their base in Kathmandu to visit their assigned villages and returning in the late afternoon. The author was asked to evaluate the work of this group and Bikas had arranged for us to meet up at the base compound at 6.30am. When I arrived, I found that the other five project managers had set off but that there was no sign of Bikas. As I came to learn, he was inclined to make his own arrangements and he had left earlier.

When we eventually caught up, Bikas explained that he did not need a motorbike. Unlike his colleagues, he chose to walk. 'Is that not a waste of your time', I asked, 'walking from one village to the next?' He looked in disbelief at the man who had been sent 7,000 miles as an advisor to help him do his job better. Then he explained:

> I will soon be walking down the track to my first village, probably with a villager who is headed in the same direction. As we walk we will discuss the project in his village. They will tell me about progress, the village news and of the reactions of villagers to the changes and how well they were being adopted. By the time I arrive at a village, I will have collected most of the information, views and opinions from villagers [or 'my customers' as he put it].

> 'I call my role here that of "facipulator" he said. (He explained that he used this word to describe how he engaged with people, using a combination of manipulation and facilitation.)

> I usually don't stop but continue walking through one village and on my way to the next. The resident village project co-ordinator walks with me and we discuss and agree actions and priorities. Then we separate and I carry on to the next villages. In between meeting people, I stop briefly for something to eat and I am usually back in the compound here before the others return on their motorbikes in the late afternoon.

A comparison of the role of project manager, as perceived by Harry and by Bikas, reveals some insight into the variations of project management practice. A surface impression would reveal the methodology, tools and techniques being followed. But in the case of Bikas there was much more to his behaviour as a player. His preoccupation lay first in a consideration of how he should conduct his work most productively to accomplish the required outcomes; in particular the way that he engaged with his customers. Bikas was distinguished from his colleagues by a continual re-examination of his working practices, their purpose and his purposefullness. His tactics were astute and focused on project outcomes and the most effective means of achieving them.

It is also important to recognise the willingness of the programme's director in Kathmandu in allowing Bikas the freedom to perform in the way of his own devising. This brought great value to his project's performance. Later, methods of project deployment used in other countries by this development charity were improved through the example pioneered in Kathmandu.

Individual-Centric or Group-Centric Performance Improvement

In Japan the need for 'acting in concert', where a group seeks to work in a new way and to spread this as innovative behaviour, has resulted in the development of 'ba'. This, loosely translates as 'place' and can occur in a group that is facilitating the adoption of new behaviours and practices for wide application in an organisation (Nonaka and Konnu, 1998).

For followers of occidental traditions ('the west'), the concern for work performance commonly begins with the competence and development of individuals; typified for example by the emphasis on 'talent management', professional qualifications and in the case of project management, familiarity with a body of knowledge and competences. Professional bodies give less attention to organisational performance and the local application of professional practices.

In an oriental culture, the working group is seen more as an accountable object (Ruch, 1984). In such a regime, players expect one another to accept an obligation to comply with, contribute and participate in the achievement of performance, learning and development.

The two traditions present profound differences in the development of an organisation and its behaviour, and for cultural reasons an understanding or emulation of these behaviours of one tradition by the other can be perplexing. Yet a comparison of these traditions does present some inspiration to explore and decide ways to improve an organisation's engagement, collaboration and pace of progress.

Patterns of Decision-Making in a Project Regime

The way that project players contribute to and share responsibility for decision-making has received little attention in the wider project management community, with the exception of studies into the behaviour of medical teams

(Pinto and Pinto, 1990). Across sectors and cultural arenas there is wide disparity in the patterns of the devolution of responsibility, involvement, creativity, consultation, collaboration and escalation. In many domains, decisions tend to be confined to project managers, sponsors and other executives. In others cases – for instance in the application of 'agile' methods (see Chapter 5) – issues are widely shared; drawing ideas from throughout a regime's community. The protocols, patterns and styles of players' engagement in a project group are typically formulated uniquely and are arranged in a way that suits organisational preferences and norms.

The extent of a regime's autonomy has a profound influence over the patterns of its decision-making. The levels of management discretion and their allocation to the project manager, project sponsor and senior management in an established project management function is a major factor determining its capacity to adapt to challenges and changes. While the decisions of all business functions are subject to the scrutiny and approval of their senior managers, in very many organisations the oversight to which the function of project management is subjected is closer, more regular and even more intrusive than that experienced by other functions. This may also be attributable to senior manager's ignorance of the circumstances of project management and the assessment of it. It may also be because the function is seen to be vulnerable to adverse risk or to be professionally immature.

Some organisations practise a policy towards exchanging information that restricts information on a 'need to know' basis. Many however, now recognise the need for greater openness in seeking to build an enterprise that places more emphasis on the wider involvement and empowerment of players. Securing a stronger capability in this way of course depends on more skilful managing, leading as well as nurturing of a work culture that is conducive to being responsive and agile. To improve a project's the tempo or pace of progress, continual adaptation relies on local discretion and decision-making.

Connection through Conversation

Social engagement, with its opportunities for rich and productive conversation enables conduct that is more assured. Without a vigorous and thorough exchange with candour and insights derived from conversation, issues and transactions can be easily overlooked or even side-lined; compromising arrangements and bringing disruption. Connection through conversation is a primary means for uncovering issues, sharing resolve and scrutiny and establishing a readiness for change.

In a mature project management community, dialogue goes beyond routine responses and enters the rigours of 'what if?', 'how can that be?', 'do we really understand this?', 'let's try' and 'how well can we anticipate the downsides?'. From such conversation, with its opportunities for appreciative enquiry (Cooperrider et al., 2008), deduction and productive argument enable a wider exploration of issues and possibilities. Conversation extends and corroborates people's thinking and enables a wider bandwidth of dialogue.

As a feature of project management practice, dialogue is too often under-played at the expense of the venture, its reliability and the pace of progress. As Theodore Zelda says, 'The possibilities of what can be done cannot be done alone'. Jürgen Habermas, the social philosopher, offers a cogent argument in his idea of 'communicative rationality'. His proposition is that the capacity for reasoning cannot be separated from dialogue and that the term 'communicative rationality' conveys the idea that dialogue is crucial to any process of reasoning (Fultner, 2011). This can be understood more easily in the narrative from *The Heretic's Guide to Best Practices* (Culmsee and Awati, 2011).

In that book, Culmsee and Awati propose that a pre-requisite for a shared understanding is 'open dialogue'. Dialogue defined here as being free from politics, strategic behaviours and power games.

Habermas's five conditions for open dialogue are:

- *Inclusion*: all affected stakeholders should be included in the dialogue.

- *Autonomy*: all participants should be able to present their viewpoints and debate those of others independently.

- *Empathy*: participants must be willing to listen to viewpoints that may be different from theirs and seek to understand them.

- *Power neutrality*: differences in status or authority levels should not influence the discussion.

- *Transparency*: participants need to be honest when presenting their views or discussing those of others.

Culmsee and Awati also refer to the circumstances that enable open dialogue as a 'holding environment'. Although a holding environment as characterised above may seem improbable, a partnership or alliance-based approach to projects can possibly provide the conditions necessary (see 'Andrew Field' in Chapter 1). An alliance-based approach to projects is where the stakeholders agree to share 'pain and gain': to work collaboratively to achieve mutually agreed goals to share both risks and rewards using an agreed formula. Also see the Centre for Collaborative Contracting (Alliancing Association, 2013).

A holding environment may also be available to a regime seeking connection and collaboration if they have the capacity to position political matters, strategic behaviours and power games aside to conduct a more open dialogue. Able conversation can bring inspiration to project players. In the book *Crucial Conversations* the authors say the following:

> *Actually the effects of conversations gone bad can be both devastating and far-reaching. Our research has shown that strong relationships, careers, organisations and communities all draw from the same source of power – the ability to talk openly about high stakes, emotional and controversial topics (Patterson et al., 2002: 9).*

Conversation can be expected to reveal insights into a project's constraints and possibilities that can otherwise be overlooked and maybe threaten progress at a later time. A more deliberate and planned approach to conversation can be expected to pay dividends. It is interesting to reflect on the extent of care often invested in preparing for a formal presentation and to contrast this with the extent of preparation conducted for, what it is expected to be a critical meeting or conversation.

Stephen Fry, the British humourist, in a 2012 BBC radio programme on the subject of conversation, spoke of it resembling 'improvised jazz' – referring to the occasional habit of 'composing on the spot' and coming up with melodies 'off the top of one's head'. There are occasions when valuable ideas or observations emerge as a conversation or dialogue enters a reflective mode; with people 'sparking off' one another. Such circumstances can produce insight and novel ideas which it is often difficult or impossible later for those present to attribute to any individual. Scrutiny for value and practicality must of course follow.

A strong and reliable community can have a steadying influence and be a source of humour, inspiration and mobilisation. But depending on the nature of such forces and the values shared, a working culture can also reveal itself as conservative; sometimes resisting innovation and organisational change (see Chapter 7).

Community behaviour in a project regime can stimulate synergies of effort; detect issues early and bring strength and clarity in its responses. Sustaining a concerted deployment of tools, terminology, culture, politics and the players' leadership also enables more effective communication and engagement within a project group and in its interactions and collaboration with other groups.

The mutualisation of responsibility and collaboration between groups relies on their maturity. Players can assume roles that are more conducive to the pace of progress; providing support to colleagues. Risks attributable to the conduct of a regime and its players are reduced and this can be of particular value when the stakes are high. Also this way, leaders become better placed to resolve disagreements.

A project community needs time to reflect on its own experiences, to accumulate wisdom and acumen. After all, its values are acquired from the positions that the players have taken in the past in their interactions and responses to events. They draw from a history that will have included triumph as well as adversity and failure. The resolution of argument and ill-feeling that can occur, if mitigated through able counsel and facilitation, can inject positive values and attitudes into the players' subsequent awareness and motivation. They provide a regime with its own place and points for reference; easing the resolution of issues and conversations that follow.

When a project regime can accumulate these positive principles and lessons over time, they serve the organisation's memory and culture, strengthening the regime and its 'cultural anchor'. This will assist a regime when addressing professional dilemmas, a difference of opinion or a clash of interests, or when contrasting attitudes that prove to be adversarial, stubborn or persistent.

Courtesy Has a Purpose

> *Courtesy is as much a mark of a gentleman as courage (Theodore Roosevelt (1858–1919), 26th US President).*

It is through their courtesy that someone can most readily demonstrate respect, appreciation and collegiality – whoever they are and whatever the circumstances of their meeting. When genuinely expressed, there will be courage and always some satisfaction. On those occasions when tensions are raised and confidence is dented, courtesy can heal the moment and strengthen the later possibilities for useful interaction and social engagement.

I know a very successful project manager who has been known to travel extensively and specifically to meet players face to face to discuss and resolve issues, before they aggravate and fester: potentially putting a venture into reverse. His style is one of courtesy and persistence and he often reflects on how much players and he learn from this practice and its outcomes.

Diligence of Dialogue

In managing a project, contention arises from ideas, views and the intentions expressed. They are, endemic to all ventures. Through dialogue they must be explored to highlight constraints and opportunities and to resolve them. All this falls to a project regime and its leadership.

Dialogue should serve as a form of moderation; reinforcing the value of experience, courtesy and insight while lessening the extremes of differences. It needs to be applied to many arenas of a project: in social engagement, collaboration, negotiation, application of rigour, programme alignment, accommodation, persistence and adaptation. As dialogue proceeds, connections will be made that will help raise the project's pace of progress (see Chapter 6).

The risks of misunderstandings, power play, disruptive arguments and disorder can be substantial. As diversions, they can distract dialogue away from its productive course. Moderating these risks, often crucial to a project, can be recognised as one of two kinds: *step-by-step* or *incremental*, as explained below.

STEP-BY-STEP

These two methods – one, QFD and two, Dialogue Mapping – are formal and serve to 'carry the dialogue'. They assist a group to achieve a closer understanding and create opportunities for resolving differences by examining common ground. They also call on players' social engagement to openly declare each of their positions.

I   Quality Function Deployment (QFD) (Clargo, 2002)

Any project has a number of objectives to accomplish and a number of choices available as actions to achieve them. A plan of what is to be done and how it is to be done has to be decided. QFD provides a way for a group of players to arrive at a consensus of the priorities.

For example, consider a project regime that wishes to improve its performance capability. The objectives may include improvements to its methods of execution, enhancement to its information systems, compliance with regulations, cost control and the players' ability to adapt. Its options as to the methods that it can use to realise these objectives may include changes to working practices; partnership with other organisations; capital investment; retaining talented personnel; working closer and more regularly with customers and users and changing some of the player's roles and responsibilities.

These objectives and the choice of methods to achieve them are important aspects of shaping, scoping and planning a project. The improvement goals and methods are set as the dimensions of a matrix. Each cell is considered by players; judging the importance of every objective and every method of implementing it. Each member of the group is expected, through dialogue, to consider the project's objectives and then to decide the relative importance of each method in realising each objective. Players' 'votes' are recorded and the matrix, once completed, provide the basis of a strategy to raise, in this case, the capability of the project regime. Conducting a QFD exercise is simple to comprehend but usually needs to be facilitated by a third party.

2   Dialogue Mapping (Conklin, 2006) or Issues-Based Information Systems (IBIS)

This is a process conducted in a workshop setting in which a diagram is developed that 'maps' a group's dialogue, capturing and connecting the players' remarks as the conversation unfolds. It is a tool for building a shared understanding and benefits from the efficacy of a shared language and dynamic conversation. Dialogue mapping is suited to working with 'wicked problems' – complex, ill-defined problems that involve multiple stakeholders (Rittel and Webber) – that are subject to social or political complexity. It can be used when attempts to find meaningful and cost effective ways of proceeding are found to be frustrated. The process tracks progress and decisions and this traces the positions and arguments that produces a record of a rigorous dialogue. The method seeks to encourage a collective deliberation of issues to arrive at a solution that is acceptable to the group.

Additional benefits of using IBIS (Werner, 1970) in a group setting can include:

- adding clarity to a discussion;

- providing a simple discussion summary;

- capturing the decision rationale;

- a common point of reference that tracks the dialogue.

INCREMENTAL

It is useful here to return to Schön's 'swampy lowlands' (Schön, 1983). A project regime can find itself in circumstances for which no one has a useful experience or ideas to offer, where there are too few principles or models that can set the direction of a dialogue and when there is confusuion or mis-trust. The issues that it faces can only be resolved through their imagination, learning, persuasion, common cause, reasoning, courtesy, engagement, candour and persistence. The efficacy of the dialogue relies upon personal attributes, resolve and the quality of connections. In this account of a critically important project meeting, its disruptions and its recovery, 'diligence of dialogue' saves the day.

Humour and Candour Matter

I recently attended a project meeting where the participants were unable to prevent the exchange of opposing views and interests from bringing negotiations to a halt. The result was frustration and resentment in abundance. Fortunately one of the participants saw fit to introduce a new approach to our predicament. Her contribution was crucial to the survival and eventually to the success of an important meeting. Her astute questioning did the trick, prompting fresh connections and engagement through her welcome humour and candour.

Seemingly single-handedly, she shifted the meeting into it acquiring a positive outlook. As I listened to her I sensed courageous intent, a clear insight into the dynamics in the group, well-developed social skills and the respect that she showed towards members of the group, which was reciprocated. In my experience this kind of skilled and brave contribution can be key to the recovery of a dialogue that has deteriorated. Insightful questions that were skilfully presented encouraged engagement, appreciation and respect for different ways of interpretation and thinking. When someone is prepared to risk a rebuff as a price worth paying, they become an agent of accommodation. This is 'venturesome' behaviour. The joint working that can be facilitated can be simply described, but it is not easy to accomplish. There can be no greater capability for a project organisation than the successful cultivation and harnessing of venturesome behaviour that enables stakeholders to seize the agenda.

Project ventures are it seems, too often in need of such resolve and conviction. Thoughtful curiosity is sometimes sporadic. Cultural habits and familiar styles of thinking can be allowed to inhibit players from 'taking the ball and running with it'. Reports of high project failure rates are often the result of propositions that have not been scrutinised with the necessary objectivity, involvement, rigour and determination. Progress becomes sluggish, with players failing to see, connect and inspire. But competition has today become keener, funding sources tighter and the consequences of failure more acute. Markets are demanding that project professionals have greater resolve, skill and courage for building rapport and resolving the inevitable differences and challenges that occur in managing a project.

Players in their groups need a strong Engagement Capability (see later in this chapter). They also need to be politically adept at maintaining a robust alliance while holding other positions beyond their project management responsibilities, claiming their time and attention. A Diligence of Dialogue is crucial to project delivery, but never simple to accomplish. The more successful professionals:

- place high value on their capacity for social interaction and engagement;

- separate matters substantial from matters circumstantial;

- consistently seek an understanding and commitment that can be shared;

- devote themselves to sense-making and continuous enquiry into the purpose of players and the means of their engagement;

- value an impartial and skilful chairperson, sometimes using the services of a facilitator who can be relied upon to be skilful and disinterested;

- seek to be informed regarding the role, motives, relationships, disposition and interests of every player.

Some key words: face; candour; persistence, bravery; respect; emotional intelligence; appreciative inquiry; empathy; comprehension and articulation; facilitation; responsibility; safe place; conversation; humour; trust; preparation; insistence; courtesy; affirmation; encounter; assent; alignment; resolute; defiant; respectful; clarity of goals; a record of progress; key issues.

In 2009 the APM People SIG (special interest group) conducted a survey of communication in project regimes. It highlighted some important findings that showed that:

- 35 per cent of project managers find initiating a communication to be 'labour-intensive' or frustrating.

- 57 per cent report that they fail to receive critical project information.

- 81 per cent consider it important or critical to receive information from colleagues; however, only 68 per cent consider it as important or critical to provide colleagues with similar information.

- 26 per cent of projects used memos or paper-based methods of communication, although none of the respondents thought these were effective.

A capacity for diversity is an asset to a project regime. This survey revealed the limitations to community behaviour in some of today's project regimes. The evidence is that while players expect to be kept informed by their colleagues, they themselves recognise that they give too little attention to keeping others informed. Social Engagement and collaboration in a project regime depends on its player's regular dialogue and this includes general conversation to link and connect, as well as communication prompted by a prescription, an established process or procedure. Should we put this down simply to a mis-understanding of the role of the project player, their professional inattention, lethargy, inadequate leadership, a symptom of an immature practice or something that is more profound or even alarming?

It is not uncommon for project players to be excluded from proceedings where they could have been expected to contribute knowledge and a point of view. Personal advantage for more senior players is sometimes acquired in this way instead of harnessing its use for strengthening opportunity and widening participation. Able people keen to share their experience and needing to learn more are sometimes left excluded – to know their place and to be confined to it.

Players are sometimes regarded by their seniors as 'cogs in the machinery' and a 'resource'. Such attitudes exclude the gains available from diversity and the development of a regime (Page, 2007). Any suggestion that this practice of holding back on opportunities for professional development is to ensure good order, should be declared by project professionals as unacceptable.

The pursuit of diversity should be regarded as routine and regular; requiring project players to offer leadership as an implicit aspect of their role. The value of people, resources, ideas, time and opportunity are easily wasted when a working culture accepts low levels of zest and determination as OK.

But such behaviour sometimes goes unchallenged. Eager players can find themselves expected to be, at significant cost to themselves, deliberately excluded from participation in dialogue – surely something that able and progressive professionals rightly regard as their due. I am referring here again to the 'paradigm paradox' (see Chapter 7). Such detachment in a community dulls the edges of discovery, learning, decision-making and the quality of endeavour.

The 'autonomy of endeavour' refers to the assignment of a task to a group of players who then accept their responsibility for its completion alongside the objectives for the pursuit of improvement. In managing projects, where players are often transitory, assigned part-time or not co-located, regime behaviour needs to be understood as it applies in a 'community of practice' (Wenger, 1998) (see later in this Chapter). Such irregular and indefinite forms of organisation typify a capable project regime. Players should not see their role to be confined to established working arrangements, but must find and build associations and activities to suit the circumstances as they find them.

A project regime as an autonomous community, cannot be reliant on prescribed processes or structures as can a line-of-business organisation. It has to rely more on regular and sustained leadership; to choose the routes to be followed and to exploit them. The sources of leadership in many organisations are now widening to include what can be called 'emergent leadership' where the work of appointed leaders is supplemented by leadership as it emerges from the ranks of junior professional players. This reflects the trends for wider and deeper involvement of professionals in sharing responsibility for undertaking and managing work. Such behaviour is also stimulated by expectations for self-management and 'agile' practices (see below). For project regimes to connect and thrive, ideas need to be championed and reasoned before then being considered for adoption.

Senior leaders and managers need to recognise that their role includes the nurturing of new ideas and their champions; for them to enjoy a freedom to perform. The role of manager as an enabler is of greater value than a mechanism to moderate player's ingenuity. Perhaps of equal importance are the social trends and cost constraints that oblige employers to promote 'employee engagement' (Walker, 2012), delegating responsibilities and empowering their staff: measures intended to attract, develop and retain the talent and initiatives of people. Members of a project regime need to be encouraged to moderate their pursuit of personal gain to recognise the satisfaction available from social engagement, collaboration, personal recognition, participation in a community, project success and advancement.

As it makes its way across virgin territory serving multiple interests and demands, a project's progression often takes players into roles beyond those that were formally assigned as the result of changing circumstances, opportunities and constraints. In order for the regime to be robust to this roller-coaster, players need to be agile in their accommodation of multiple perspectives and be well informed about current developments. An employment contract, both psychologically and contractually needs to reflect this.

Dynamic Linking or Connected Autonomy

Project management depends upon the harnessing of initiatives through their connection within purpose and goals that are subject to change. Promoting the efforts of teams that retain some autonomy while at the same time maintaining coherent progress, can be assisted by a pattern of working known as 'dynamic linking' (Denning, 2010). A reporting structure alone is often found deficient for providing the connections needed by project management. Initiatives need to be combined and interlinked firmly and continually in other ways. The method began in automotive design in Japan and has been developed more fully in software development with methods known as 'Agile'.

Dynamic linking in a project regime is characterised by:

- work being undertaken in short cycles;

- managers setting priorities in terms of the work goals based on what is known about what is most likely to satisfy stakeholders;

- decisions about the work needing to be done to achieve those goals are made to be the responsibility of those doing the work;

- progress being measured (to the extent possible) by direct client feedback at the end of each cycle.[1]

Connecting through Social Engagement

A project regime is more than a set of roles, responsibilities and reporting relationships. These factors are important but are entirely insufficient as a definition of an organisation. A capable regime is equipped to devise and adapt working arrangements as these become necessary as the project evolves. Effective organisation also relies on the experience of its players and the values and practices of it as a community. Serial planning will continually re-set the agenda for what is to be done and how; project work is conducted on a stage where, through its resolve, dialogue and organisation, players devise tasks and adapt them as necessary to ensure successful execution and delivery.

Many project tasks are devised and conducted for the first time: that is in the nature of projects. It will be the players' thinking, engagement, decision-

---

1   Dynamic linking is a term derived from software design. A compiler automatically invokes the linker as the last step in compiling a program. The linker inserts code (or maps in shared libraries) to resolve program library references and/or combines object modules into executable code.

making and collaboration that will execute and deliver what is required. The enterprise has to be purposeful; inspiring the adaptation of players as individuals and as groups.

Players need to work as members of an 'actor network' (Hodder, 2012), converging their efforts through joint action. Able and proficient players have to sustain their agility. In the more accomplished project regimes, its capability has been acquired over a period through venturesome and mature endeavour.

In this fast-growing and still nascent occupation, it is a minority of project regimes that have the maturity that is actually required. Many players, as individuals and as groups, have yet to comprehend their full potential. When mature; a project management community is fully conversant with its subject and domain, able to project a clear project management identity and having formed robust relationships with customers, sponsors, stakeholders and suppliers.

In a shifting and competitive globalised world that demands business critical responses, adaptation and agility have become imperatives. Project organisations will thrive only if they have the capacity for swift and sure adaptation: enough for progress, profitability and competitive advantage.

But there is a need for caution here. Responses to immediate demands of the project however important, cannot be allowed to threaten the integrity and coherence of a project regime. A regime's structures of roles, responsibilities, planning and the schedule, method, regular dialogue and resolve, serve as guardians of order and integrity. These elements, the 'Essential Schemas' (see Figure 5.1), are arrangements that if abused will compromise the vital good order of things. Structures are crucial; from which players can step away when adapting to circumstances to then be returned and found to be intact. Progress relies on maintaining a balance between the Human and Organisational Capabilities (HOCs) and the Methodological and Operational Capabilities (MOCs) (see Figure 5.1).

A project regime deploys working groups of players to undertake tasks. These groups need to behave capably: continually shaping what is to be done, how it will be done and the pace at which it is done. Players need to act concertedly, to be tolerant of ambiguity and to accommodate the uncertainties of their work.

A project regime will sometimes be observed as irrational or even disordered. Conduct can appear to be 'a mess' to some observers, while to others the turmoil will be evidence of talent, creative problem-solving and the continual consideration of fresh routes to progress and improvement. Project management is an expedition that must continually search for routes that are more productive – relying on the players' observations, curiosity, endurance and essential leadership. A project regime is itself a primary source of risks that can lead to triumph but also to catastrophe and to everything in between.

Groups of project players can be small or large, virtual or extant, peripatetic or permanent, appointed as a task-force or arising spontaneously. And, whereas in a past era standard procedures and gateways were regarded as setting a regime's base-line, a 'more-of-the-same' attitude is less likely to suit the enterprises of today with their sponsors' mandate for adaptation and continuous improvement. Venturesome groups must have the capacity to engage in concert; exploiting the diversity, perspectives and informed decision-making that only social engagement can provide.

Social Engagement and Engagement Goals

A work group can, through its understanding and application of Engagement Goals (Figure 4.2), be more confident of securing productive pathways to a

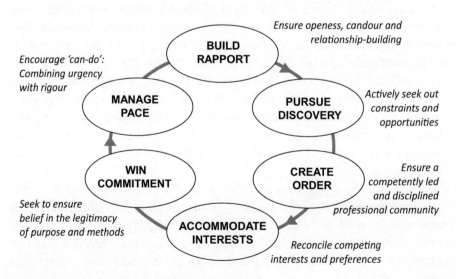

Figure 4.2   A Regime's Engagement Goals
Source: 2012 © EngagementWorks Ltd.

project's progress. A group's objectives are formulated and realised through its experience, thinking, dialogue and social engagement. The value of the Engagement Capability of a work group is its leverage of social capital that can be achieved from the collaboration that it can then enable. Engagement Capability is created and sustained from the collective abilities and diligence of a group's members; not available from any individual member.

The descriptions of Engagement Goals below each include a list of 'Behaviours to Build'. They are not exclusive to any one goal, but the lists help to characterise each goal and provide a point of reference for devising learning objectives for the development of a regime's capability. The six Engagement Goals are described on the following pages.

I BUILD RAPPORT

Rapport emerges from openness, candour and strong relationships. When we watch people working together and finding themselves to be 'on the same wavelength' we are witnessing rapport: sensing a mode or atmosphere that makes it more possible to reach a common understanding and commitment. In this way players work more openly, examine and explore ideas, challenge one another, conduct joint problem-solving and secure a common intention. Misunderstandings and conflict can be more easily avoided and, when they do occur, responses can be expected to be more reliable in producing a practical outcome. When rapport is weak, social interaction and communication will have been compromised along with everything else.

Rapport can sometimes follow a successful exchange of contrasting and keenly held opinion, with the protagonists claiming to have experienced a 'clearing of the air' yielding some mutual respect. From a rigorous negotiation, the encounter can serve to introduce a 'rapport refresh'. It seems the richest manifestations of rapport are those that are the result of a shared emotional experience or a 'feel-good' mutual dependence.

Rapport between people may grow over time and vestiges of an association can be retained over long periods, making it possible to 'pick up' with someone after a gap of years. Rapport makes it possible to build the foundations of a community and its culture that provides inclusive, personal and social connections. People enjoying the company of others and the humour that it offers can bring close rapport and this can become the basis of rich conversation, association and, in project management, more reliable and swifter progress.

When the stakes are high, rapport can permit greater candour; making it possible for people to engage more openly and productively. In *Crucial Conversations* (Patterson et al., 2002) the authors refer to the idea of a 'safe place' where such behaviour becomes possible when the threat to confidentiality, security or personal reputation is removed. Achieving this level of understanding and trust between players can to the sceptic, appear as a fantasy. But when social engagement achieves high levels level of rapport, the freedom of exchange that it affords has often been hard-won. This can be an indication of commitment, professional ambition, resolve and community maturity (see Chapter 4).

Project players must be able to win rapport in a variety of situations, including when there is disagreement or a low level of mutual regard. This is where the ability to express leadership and humour are key professional assets.

Rapport-building between people who do not share a common language need to handle cultural differences with care. When there is sensitivity to authority, there will always be a challenge to anyone exercising leadership. Simple courtesy can go a long way to reduce these barriers to rapport.

Behaviours to Build Rapport

✓   Appreciative inquiry.

✓   Active listening.

✓   Emotional intelligence.

✓   Employee engagement (with the purpose and methods of their employer).

✓   Conviction that a close working relationship is required.

✓   The desire in people to get to know others and to become conversant.

✓   Sharing common values.

✓   Sharing common experiences and acquaintances.

✓   Mutual respect (real and as enacted).

✓   The pursuit of mutual trust.

✓   Courtesy.

✓   A 'safe place'.

✓   Empathy.

✓   People exercising their authority to learn.

✓   The courage to confront people and issues.

✓   Skilful use of language and rhetoric.

2   PURSUE DISCOVERY

To be progressive, a project regime has to be continuously looking out for circumstances that need its attention, such as:

- New or revised requirements or changes to scope.

- Supply chain difficulties and opportunities.

- More experienced professionals as players.

- Developments in stakeholders' circumstances.

- Factors that will yield greater customer satisfaction.

- Advance notice of a likely constraint.

- Advance notice of a likely opportunity.

- Changing the pace of progress (see Chapter 6).

Initially, a discovery is likely to be recognised as a constraint or an opportunity but as the project proceeds, the dynamics and unpredictability of an enterprise can reverse that assessment, with players recognising that an earlier assessment has proved to have been incorrectly assumed. For example, when a cost reduction measure serves to threaten a project activity, component or feature, it can sometimes lead not only to some economy, but this ingenuity can then introduce a superior alternative. A capable project regime will seek to turn apparent constraints into opportunities while at the same time building on existing opportunities. An attentive regime, or one that is inattentive, can be its own architect of its fate.

A good example of this comes from the story describing the discovery of what is today known as the microprocessor. Some work by Intel with ETI, a now defunct Japanese company, specified a project for developing solid-state electronics to power a new generation of desk calculators. ETI had designed 12 calculator 'chips' and had asked Intel to manufacture them. Intel's Federico Faggin was assigned the project and after studying the designs he concluded that the potential of their complexity far exceeded the functions required of a calculator. He had realised that a general-purpose programmable processor would be a simpler design, yet able to handle a greater number of functions. The Intel 4004 was thus conceived. In 1969 ETI chose Intel's 'microcomputer on a chip' (the word microprocessor wasn't used until 1972) over its own 12-chip design.

Discovery is both the heartbeat and a threat to a project enterprise. When resources are low or competition threatens, adversity – self-inflicted or imposed – can be the mother of invention and creativity.

A project needs over-the-horizon radar to see issues approaching. Information when presented early can confer huge benefits. Judicious networking should be deploying pickets to bring such early warning. Something in the style and disposition of a project regime's most able professionals help them to grow a strong network of people inclined to pass-on and share implications and possibilities.

A forewarning of discovery cannot be expected. But once the value or significance of a discovery becomes evident, greater benefits to the project emerge in its exploitation. It pays for the curiosity players to question stakeholders and others with an interest in the enterprise. Examining possibilities that have the potential to be beneficial can be worthwhile even at a time when a link may not then seem to be likely.

Behaviours to Build Discovery

✓   Abiding curiosity.

✓   Active listening and conversation.

✓   A desire to be successful.

✓   Diligent networking.

✓   Openness to the unexpected or unfamiliar.

✓   Openness to possibilities and their assessment.

✓   Thorough comprehension of the client's/sponsor's perception of the project.

✓   Scepticism.

✓   Emotional intelligence.

✓   The courage to venture.

✓   Anticipating mid-course corrections.

✓   A focus on execution, added value and extension.

✓   Political acumen.

✓   Close rapport with stakeholders.

✓   Sensitivity to the real needs of the customer, user and end-user.

✓   Watching out for champions and allowing them space.

3   CREATE ORDER

To function effectively players depend on a regime's sense and pursuit of order. Two inter-related aspects to this are the orderliness of working arrangements and the orderliness of players' behaviour. Attempts at managing the complexities of a project can be undermined when players are unable to 'keep their house in order'.

Orderliness depends on the richness of a regime's legacy of professional good practice and on hard-headed responses to a project's demands; both immediate and strategic. We examine below some aspects of a regime's working arrangements and behaviour as factors that determine the quality of a regime's orderliness.

The orderliness of working arrangements are managed through a set of protocols that include those concerning:

1.   A common understanding of and commitment to mission and goals.

2.   Partnership with the sponsor(s).

3.   Players remaining clear about their roles and responsibilities and those of their colleagues, despite continual adaptations by the project as to what is to be achieved and how.

4.   Alignment with a programme and portfolio.

5.   Preservation of a regime's autonomy.

6.   Attention to the pace of progress.

7.   The capacity for adaptation to changes.

8.   Assuring attention to the inter-dependence of work-streams.

9.   Communication – both broadcast and conducted locally between players.

10. Leadership that sets the tone and addresses issues promptly.

11. Information systems that meet their requirements.

12. Decision-making, planning, method, methodology, control and record-keeping.

The orderliness of behaviour managed through a set of protocols that include those concerning:

1.   Pursuit of collective intention and resolve.

2.   Acceptable and unacceptable social interaction.

3.   Professional development of players.

4.   Promotion of community behaviour and its maturity.

5.   Social engagement, conversation and collaboration.

6.   A culture that meets the necessities of the regime.

7.   Accommodation of dissent and disruption.

8.   Respect for the opinions and preferences of players.

9.   Players' leadership in responding to events and practices.

10.   Support to players when experiencing adversity.

11.   Prompt mediation in the event of disagreement.

12.   The obligation on all players to act as custodians of order.

The existence of a 'Cultural Anchor' in a community that is widely regarded and well understood, can provide points of reference for players and a foundation for good order. It can govern many aspects of the values and behaviour of players. John P. Kotter uses the term cultural anchor as Step 8: Make it Stick in his book *Leading Change*. He says:

> *New practices must grow deep roots to remain firmly planted in the culture. Culture is composed of norms of behaviour and shared values. These social forces are incredibly strong. Every individual that joins an organization is indoctrinated into its culture, generally without even realizing it. Its inertia is maintained by the collective group of employees over years. Changes – whether consistent or inconsistent with the old culture – are difficult to ingrain (Kotter, 2012).*

For long-standing project regimes, orderliness can sustain constancy by reference to its cultural anchor, but leaders must be wary when challenging convention or seeking to modify cultural norms. For young and nascent regimes, cultural norms are more plastic and the benefits of an anchor (and its constraints) hold less sway. In managing projects therefore the challenge lies in 'creating order' as well as maintaining it.

Behaviours to Build the Creation of Order

✓   Active listening.

✓   Courtesy and tolerance.

✓   Emotional intelligence.

✓   Respect for cultural norms.

✓   Political sensitivity.

✓   Capacity to challenge or extend cultural norms.

✓   Willingness to confront issues.

✓   Productive conversation.

✓   Respect for the cultural anchor.

✓   An expectation of challenge and innovation.

✓   Appreciative enquiry.

✓   Reasoning.

✓   Leadership that shows the way forward.

✓   The pursuit of professionalism.

✓   References to project and portfolio requirements.

✓   References to roles and responsibilities.

✓   Recognition of both team and individual behaviour.

✓   Risk awareness.

4   ACCOMMODATE INTERESTS

Stakeholders' always have interests to be pursued. These might include the protection of their proprietary rights to valuable techniques, technologies and working practices. They can also include agreements with third parties that may be breached by a prospective arrangement. In protecting their interests, a stakeholder may choose to declare them at a pre-planning stage or they may seek to hide it or announce it at a later stage, say during execution! It is not uncommon for stakeholders to recognise a conflict of interest late in the proceedings.

Stakeholder interests need to be given close attention at the shaping and scoping stage of a project. Recognising and hopefully limiting threats and downside risks and exploring the possible impact on the project, is better undertaken before they become more complex or otherwise uncertain.

Delays, oversights and misunderstandings regarding the interests of stakeholders have the potential to be very damaging to a project regime's endeavours and to professional reputations. A project regime needs to be assiduous in the identification of interests, ensure regular liaison with stakeholders and in reminding players and stakeholders of their common interest in the project's progress.

The project manager will commonly take primary responsibility for stakeholders' interests being recognised and understood and, where conflict arises, seek to accommodate them and to negotiate a reconciliation.

A process of accommodating interests bears much in common with that of seeking collaboration. In Chapter 1 the importance to collaboration of starting with the building of a shared understanding of goals, and this leading to a shared commitment to achieve them, is elaborated.

Behaviours to Build the Accommodation of Interests

✓   Initial shaping and scoping of the project and agreeing terms.

✓   All stakeholders accepting responsibility for reconciling issues affecting the conduct or purposes of a project.

✓   Continual and active project review of stakeholder objectives, conditions and interests.

✓   Early attention to any issue arising.

✓   Involvement of all stakeholders who are likely to be affected by an issue.

✓   Scepticism.

✓   Negotiation.

✓   Escalation.

✓   Appreciative enquiry.

✓   Political acumen.

✓   Reframing.

✓   Persistence.

✓   Relationship management.

✓   Methods for a regime build an accommodation of interests.

5 WIN COMMITMENT

A project is a venture in which costs, value and delivery cannot be guaranteed. Skilful project management must be expected to manage and contain downside risks and to exploit opportunities.

The commitment of project players, their determination, tenacity, resolve, dialogue and organisation will have a pervasive and positive influence on the conduct of players. It lies in the behaviour of the sponsor and project manager to mitigate the downside risks to a project and this relies on them questioning, imagining and selecting the paths to progress.

The leaders of a project endeavour must work to win the commitment of all project players and any other parties involved. For them to become committed, they must be aware of plans and issues and be free to question, express their opinion and offer their point of view. The stronger project regimes seek this behaviour from their players. Commitment by the project regime is unlikely to be sustained without it transparently being the will of the sponsor and their enterprise (the firm or public/civic authority).

Authentic commitment is more likely to be evident in the behaviour of players than in the rhetoric of advocates. What people do matters; what they say awaits a verdict redeemed by useful action. People's commitment feeds on successful behaviour as recognised in the practices of co-workers and particularly in the actions and decisions of seniors. Initiatives that struggle for attention in a regime where commitment is weak, cannot be relied upon to sustain the promised pace of progress.

Commitment manifests itself in the manner in which detailed work is undertaken and in the way that the bigger issues are resolved. And its expression can be both implicit and explicit. In the former it can be experienced in the confidence of a mature professional where on someone's enquiry, they are readily able to explain and justify their decisions and actions. The latter has its place in the behaviour of its backers, trainers, mentors and other leaders (see Cockburn, 2006). Commitment should be an element in an organisation's cultural anchor, sustaining its momentum and progress through challenging periods of adversity.

Behaviours to Build Winning of Commitment

✓ Common understanding.

✓ Candour and respect.

✓ Regular conversation and briefing.

✓ Displays of commitment and its impact on performance.

✓ Training and development.

✓ Mentoring.

✓ Acceptance of responsibility.

✓ Effective and complete documentation.

✓ Humour and irony.

✓   Proving trust.

✓   Skilful delegation.

✓   Promotion of autonomy.

✓   Celebration.

✓   Attention to well-being.

✓   The opening of career paths.

✓   Coaching and counselling.

✓   Courtesy.

✓   Strengthening of the cultural anchor.

✓   Community of practice.

✓   Fairness.

✓   Learning.

✓   Professionalism.

6   SUSTAIN PACE

A project's pace of progress is determined by its players maximising the quality and swiftness of delivery (see Chapter 6, 'The Project's Pace').

Engagement Capability: Diagnostic Tool EIQ6

Organisations wishing to improve a project regime's capability need to encourage and promote the players' social engagement: behaviour that enables working groups to connect and to deploy ideas, energy and perspectives to then be able to stimulate the project's essential collaboration. The EIQ6 tool assists players in recognising the strength of their engagement as a group in terms of its capacity to meet six engagement goals (see Figure 4.2). It is also a method for comparing the Engagement Capability of different groups. The instrument can

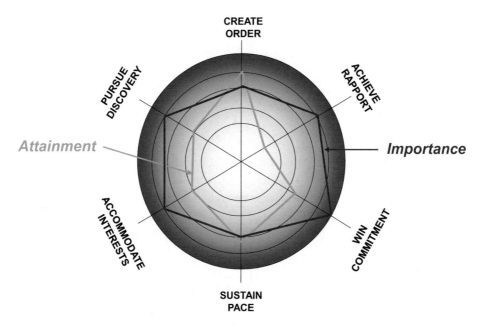

CREATE
ORDER

PURSUE
DISCOVERY

ACHIEVE
RAPPORT

Attainment **Importance**

ACCOMMODATE
INTERESTS

WIN
COMMITMENT

SUSTAIN
PACE

Figure 4.3   Assessing Engagement Capability

Source: 2012 © EngagementWorks Ltd.

be used to improve social interaction and is a powerful resource for assisting the orientation of functional specialists when acting in the role of a project player.

Figure 4.3 shows an example of an analysis produced from the EIQ6 diagnostic tool developed by EngagementWorks. The figure compares a group's assessment of its own engagement capability to attain six organisational goals, together with its own view as to the importance of each of the six in their own circumstances. In this example the group expresses the opinion that the quality of rapport in the group is weaker than they believe it to be required. It also shows that their capacity for sustaining pace and for creating order exceeds what they see to be required in their circumstances.

This diagnostic is used for a comparative assessment of Engagement Capability: over time and for comparison with other groups.

Connection and Community

Connections are described at the beginning of this chapter:

Connections serve to link and combine ideas, energy and perspectives that then enable goals and plans to be shaped and developed. A project regime progresses through purposeful and venturesome dialogue that is conducted across its network of connections. And all this is to enable robust and progressive project execution and delivery.

A genuine community can however elevate a project's capability a lot further: taking it beyond that provided by its connections, by applying single-mindedness to 'act as one' (see the story of Janet in Chapter 1, page 13). When there is community there can be collegiality and greater authenticity, candour, commitment and freedom of expression. Social engagement can then acquire a life of its own, bringing with it the prize of concerted action and the performance multiplier.

Connections can reinforce what has come to be known as the social capital of an organisation. This is defined by Robert Putnam as 'the collective value of all social networks and the inclinations that arise from such works to do things for each other'. As he notes in *Bowling Alone* (Putnam, 2000), in recent years social capital has been shrinking. In the United States he found that over the last 25 years attendance at club meetings has fallen by 58 per cent, family dinners are down 33 per cent and visiting friends has fallen by 45 per cent.

References to 'communication' as a common failure in the management of a project often serve to trivialise the complexities of activities required for what is referred to here more explicitly, as 'connection and community'. Sociologist Ray Oldenburg states in the *The Great Good Place* (1999) that people need three places to find community: the home, the workplace and the community hang-out. The contributions from a project regime's community; where what is to be done and how, is a continuous agenda and can be profound.

Attention by a project regime to its connection and community should enhance a project regime's capacity:

1.   to enhance social engagement;

2.   to enhance the ability to influence stakeholder's intentions, objectives or organisation;

3.   to conduct the management of a project as an integrated and interdependent amalgam of features and functions; and

4.   to enhance the view of a project as a collective quest more than as a means of players achieving personal ambition.

Stepping towards Community Maturity

The clearer a project regime's leaders are able to be in shaping their community, the more conducive it becomes to making project progress and improved capability. Initiatives to develop community enterprise in this way in the occident, certainly in a commercial context, are generally less frequent than they were in the past. In Britain there are many examples from the nineteenth century. These included Lever Brothers of Ellesmere Port (soap), Cadbury of Birmingham (chocolate), Titus Salt of Saltaire (woollen cloth) and Fry's of Bristol (chocolate). Such arrangements today appear to many as a 'welfare' regime in which people are being patronised. We should perhaps question whether this is the only lesson to be learned.

One of the characteristics of these enterprises in the past was the owners' promotion of an ethos and an ethic. They were often motivated by philanthropic intent. Much of the success of their businesses can be attributed to policies that provided for employees' housing, welfare and job security. Today enterprise communities have featured perhaps predominantly in Asia. In both Toyota and Samsung employee attitude, commitment and behaviours have been harnessed to the business's growth, innovation, productivity and profitability, through the promotion of a corporate credo and practices (see 'Resolute Leadership' and accounts from Samsung, Chapter 3).

Today the extent to which culture in a project regime is influential to the advantage or to the detriment of its progress varies very widely between and within projects. Also, global trading has resulted in players needing to conduct themselves as co-workers while holding different values and carrying different assumptions and behaviours.

'Employee Engagement' is a movement that seeks to persuade employers to engineer a culture that connects employees' preferences with the behaviours recognised by the employer to be contributing to enterprise and competitive advantage. It centres on the extent to which there is synergy between the motivations and satisfaction pursued by employees and the policies and preferences of the organisation where they are employed. On the website, Invigor8 (Gannon, 2013), employee engagement is explained and includes the following extract.

1.   *A Common Cause is crucial. Your business needs an agreed and aligned strategy around a clear purpose that all can sign up to. 'This is common sense', you say, but so many companies fall at this first hurdle, in fact the vast majority of organisations fail here and, significantly, this usually starts with senior teams not being rigorous enough in their strategic planning and then failing to link up the various strands and, in many cases, individuals actively working to not engage and co-operate with one another.*

2.   *Naturally high performing people are attracted to strong brands. So ensure you research your market and customers thoroughly and develop branded products and services that really do differentiate. Ensure your brand values translate in to strong experiences and emotions for customers that can be delivered by outstandingly passionate employees. More about achieving this passion shortly.*

3.   *You need to develop one strong explicit culture within the organisation (not lots of sub cultures):*

   a.   *A clear, memorable vision about where you are headed is a vital component here.*

   b.   *Next, an agreed set of internal values – expressed in every day terms that are developed by and owned by the whole business. This is a point often missed; too often values are developed by top teams on away days and then imposed on the rest of the organisation as if they came from Jupiter. Indeed, they might as well have come from there – top teams rarely speak in the language of the front line!*

   c.   *So involve your colleagues and research thoroughly.*

   d.   *Make sure the values are translated into behaviours and test them out. Do they engender enthusiasm within the work force? Do they align with your brand promise? Will they deliver a real difference for your customers – because they impact positively on all the key 'touch points' – and for you?*

By way of an analogue, the steps in the development of rowers to become members of a mature racing crew are shown in Table 4.1. It traces their learning and adaptation as a means of adopting the behaviours and competencies that characterise a community.

Table 4.1   Community Maturity: Four Steps Towards the Maturity of a Rowing Crew

Step 1	Unconscious incompetence NEW PERSONAL BEHAVIOUR	The beginner struggles with the physically unfamiliar techniques of rowing with oars. At this stage every aspect of the activity is new and the rower is unsure of what they are doing right or wrong. Rowing is a new behaviour.
Step 2	Consciously incompetent ENDORSED BEHAVIOUR	Each member of the boat's crew is now familiar with the basics of how to row and aware when they have done something right or done something wrong, although they are still unsure of what lies behind the basic techniques. The four or eight in the boat are coached and encouraged by their cox. This is endorsed behaviour.
Step 3	Consciously competent PRACTICED BEHAVIOUR	The members of the boat's crew can now move the boat through the water with reasonable speed and accuracy. This is practised behaviour.
Step 4	Unconsciously competent ACCEPTED BEHAVIOUR	The crew are now seasoned at working to row the boat together. They no longer need to concentrate on the basics of rowing and are able to adapt to the need to speed up or slow down, can plan ahead and can respond to the behaviour of competing boats. Rowing is now accepted behaviour.

In Figure 4.4, on the next page, we can see the same principles applied to the maturity of a project management regime. In the first stage, characteristic behaviour for a newly arrived player starts as 'unadopted', where they are responding to being *told* through facilitation about 'the way that we do things around here'.

This moves through to a situation in which, through some experience and guidance, players learn with others the behaviour that is valued and endorsed. The players' *training* here is more formalised and remains closely facilitated.

In the third stage these behaviours become accepted and adopted through practice, with players *striving* to adjust and adapt to a community's preferences and typical behaviour. Facilitation is at 'arm's length'.

Finally, the behaviour becomes customary, with players *naturally* behaving in sympathy with the community's culture and its players' affiliations. Much of their learning is conducted through their recall and personal reflection.

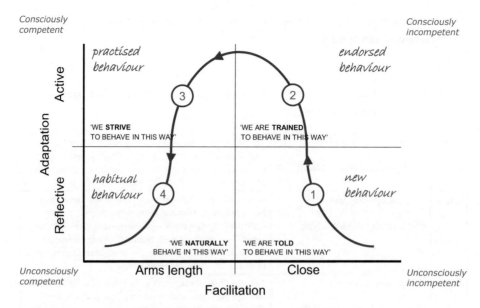

Figure 4.4   Project Community Maturity (PCM)
Source: 2012 © EngagementWorks Ltd.

The development of a regime's community maturity always follows a complex and unique course. It derives from its legacy, critical incidents and personalities, and from the experiences of leaders coping with challenges and external circumstances. A development route has to be designed with care and is 'fed' continually by new experiences.

The path described here that traces an individual's development could be used for planning the development of a work group. It can be argued that any experience that succeeds in initiating a person into a community will follow this sequence, as generally described here.

In assessing the performance and potential of a community, the stage of community maturity already reached by the people being considered should be determined. Development is always incremental; building on strengths already acquired and through an approach that is built from the existing 'asset-base'.

Professional Pointers

*   Dialogue has to serve as a form of moderation, reinforcing the value of experience and insight while lessening the extremes of differences.

- Routes to progress have first to be discovered.

- Candour cannot succeed without a receptive audience.

- Players seek connection as a base-line for collaboration.

- Build rapport.

- Pursue discovery.

- Create order.

- Accommodate interests.

- Win commitment.

- Sustain pace.

References

Alliancing Association. (2013). Retrieved from Centre for Collaborative Contracting. Available at: http://www.a3c3.org.

Awati, K. (2011). Macrovisions and micromanagement, 20 October. Available at: http://eight2late.wordpress.com.

Clargo, M. (2002). *Managing by Design: Using QFD to Transform Management Performance*. London: Tesseracts.

Cockburn, A. (2006). *Shu Ha Ri*. Available at: http://alistair.cockburn.us/Shu+Ha+Ri.

Conklin, J. (2006). *Dialogue Mapping: Building Shared Understanding of Wicked Problems*. Chichester: Wiley.

Cooperrider, D.L. and Whitney, D. (2005). *Appreciative Inquiry: A Positive Revolution in Change*. San Francisco, CA: Berrett-Koehler.

Cooperrider, D.L., Whitney, D. and Stavros, J.M. (2008). *Appreciative Inquiry Handbook: For Leaders of Change*. Brunswick, OH: Crown Custom Publishing.

Culmsee, P. and Awati, K. (2011). *The Heretic's Guide to Best Practices: The Reality of Managing Complex Problems in Organisations*. Bloomington, IN: iUniverse.

Denning, S. (2010). *Radical Management*. San Francisco, CA: Jossey-Bass.

Etzioni, A. (1995). *The Spirit of Community*. New York: Crown.

Fultner, B. (2011). *Jürgen Habermas: Key Concepts*. Durham: Acumen.

Gannon, P. (2013). *Invigor8*. Available at: http://www.invigor8.eu/serious.html [accessed 9 December 2013].

Goleman, D. (1995). *Emotional Intelligence: Why It Can Matter More than IQ*. New York: Bantam.

Hillson, D. and Murray-Webster, R. (2005). *Understanding and Managing Risk Attitude*. Aldershot: Gower.

Hodder, I. (2012). *Entangled: An Archaeology of the Relationships between Humans and Things*. Oxford: Wiley.

Kotter, J.P. (2012). *Leading Change*. Boston, MA: Harvard Business School Press.

Liker, J.K. (2004). *The Toyota Way*. New York: McGraw-Hill.

Nonaka, I. and Konnu, N. (1998). The concept of 'ba': Building a foundation for knowledge creation. *California Management Review*, 40(3): 40–54.

Oldenburg, R. (1999). *The Great Good Place: Cafés, Coffee Shops, Bookstores, Bars, Hair Salons, and Other Hangouts at the Heart of a Community*. New York: Marlowe.

Page, S.E. (2007). *The Difference: How the Power of Diversity Creates Better Groups, Firms, Schools, and Societies*. Princeton, NJ: Princeton University Press.

Patterson, K., Grenny, J., McMillan, R. and Switzler, A. (2002). *Crucial Conversations: Tools for Talking When Stakes Are High*. New York: McGraw-Hill.

Pinto, M.B. and Pinto, J.K. (1990). Project team communication and cross-functional cooperation in new program development. *Journal of Product Innovation Management*, 7(3): 200–212.

Putnam, R.D. (2000). *Bowling Alone: The Collapse and Revival of American Community*. New York: Simon & Schuster.

Rittel, H.W.J. and Webber, M.M. (1973). Dilemmas in a general theory of planning. *Policy Sciences*, 4(2): 155–69.

Ruch, W.V. (1984). *Corporate Communications: A Comparison of Japanese and American Practices*. Westport, CT: Quorum.

Schön, D. (1983). *The Reflective Practitioner*. New York: Basic Books.

Walker, S. (2012). *Employee Engagement and Communication Research*. London: Kogan Page.

Wenger, E. (1998). *Communities of Practice: Learning, Meaning, and Identity*. Cambridge: Cambridge University Press.

Werner, K. and Rittel, H.W.J. (1970). *Issues as Elements of Information Systems*. Berkeley, CA: Institute of Urban and Regional Development, University of California.

Chapter 5

The Project's Rigour

Sustaining Good Governance, Method, Orderliness and Discipline

---

Applying standards and techniques with practicality and agility to good effect. Relying on community maturity and open, rational and astute decision-making.

Refer to the Nine Crucial Capabilities

Now that we've lost sight of our objective, speed rather than direction is our highest priority.

Clausewitz

Introduction

Project management rigour is expressed by a project regime's enterprise, principles and professionalism; achieved by the excellence of its planning, methods and behaviours.

Activities are addressed comprehensively and executed through diligence, tenacity and precision; with risk and the pace of progress closely managed. The 'Aspects' model in Figure 5.1 presents the diversity of the project management discipline and shows the distinction between systematic procedures of project management (Essential Schemas) and the regime's conduct of agility (Vital Behaviours). It illustrates the eclectic quality of project management, highlighting the human and organisational factors, too often disregarded.

The Right Things, Done Right

A theatre production can be valued in two ways. The first from an appreciation of the theatre itself: the interior, lighting, sound system, seats, and the stage with its equipment. These elements are universal to any performance and are about *doing the right things* according to the directions of the theatre architect, manager and playwright.

Second, there is value in the spectacle and drama of the performance, as presented from an understanding and interpretation of the author's script and the actors' creative and dramatic contributions. These elements are particular to any performance. They are conveyed by the director interpreting and casting the parts, adapting to the venue and bringing leadership and meaning to the performance. They create and deliver a performance that emerges from the producers and players' choices of what they see to be the *right things to do*. The harmony and synergy of the two together: the theatre and the theatrical performance are evident in the quality of a performance.

Project management can be appreciated in a similar way. Methodology, metrics, the life-cycle, plans, professional standards; procedures, structures and methods prescribe ways of a project *doing things right*. These set the stage for the players through their behaviour; comprehending and interpreting the requirement, addressing issues and relationships to execute and deliver. They are responding to the stakeholder's needs to bring leadership and meaning to their venture. Their behaviour creates and delivers outcomes and products that are the result of their pursuit of what they decide to be *the right things to do*.

In Aspect A in Figure 5.1, the 'MOCs' of project management provide a framework of structures, methods, systems and procedures as the range of 'Essential Schemas' to enable support to the venture. Included in 'doing the right things', a project regime will choose the schemas to be employed. The regime has to define the scope and shape, adopt a planning process and keep track of progress. The project will also, using a range of tools and techniques, ensure financial probity and deploy information and other systems to record events, track progress, process information and ensure the necessary communication.

In Aspect B in Figure 5.1, the 'HOCs' of project management are the abilities of the players to choose to *do things right*: comprehending the project requirement and its solutions through social engagement: responding to the stakeholders, adapting to circumstances and sustaining a regime's agility. It requires resolve, analysis, dialogue, cogently argued exchanges and conversation between players

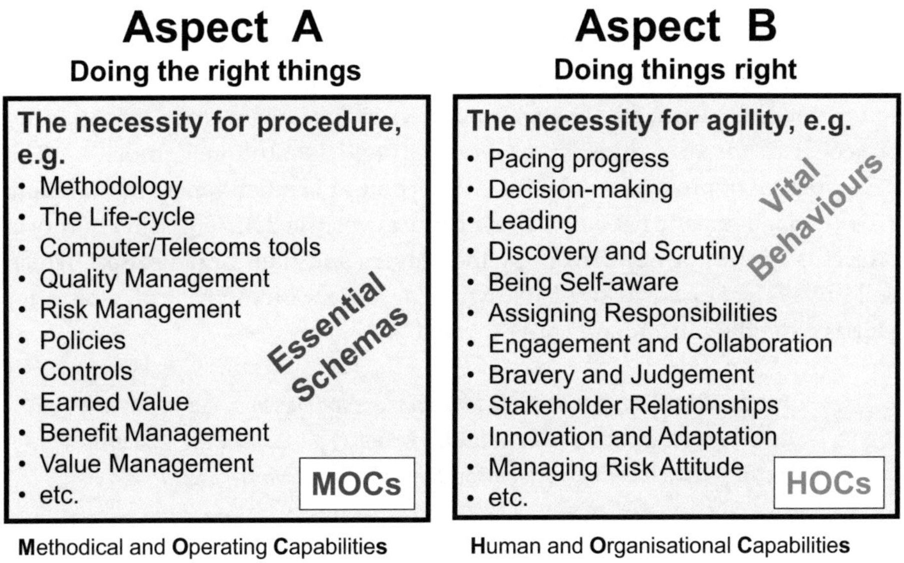

Aspect A
Doing the right things

The necessity for procedure, e.g.
- Methodology
- The Life-cycle
- Computer/Telecoms tools
- Quality Management
- Risk Management
- Policies
- Controls
- Earned Value
- Benefit Management
- Value Management
- etc.

Essential Schemas

MOCs

Methodical and **O**perating **C**apabilities

Aspect B
Doing things right

The necessity for agility, e.g.
- Pacing progress
- Decision-making
- Leading
- Discovery and Scrutiny
- Being Self-aware
- Assigning Responsibilities
- Engagement and Collaboration
- Bravery and Judgement
- Stakeholder Relationships
- Innovation and Adaptation
- Managing Risk Attitude
- etc.

Vital Behaviours

HOCs

Human and **O**rganisational **C**apabilities

Figure 5.1   Complete Project Management – Two Aspects
Source: 2012 © EngagementWorks Ltd.

and stakeholders, skilful organisation and being astute and venturesome. Project work needs the attention of mature project professionals and players working as a community to lead members through oversight, productive thinking, adaptation, social engagement and collaboration.

Perhaps most importantly, HOCs include the abilities to exercise the ingenuity needed to maintain and improve the pace of progress (see Chapter 6) through the regime's resolve, dialogue and organisation. As defined here, MOCs provide a framework of systematic tools and methodology to ensure good order. The HOCs bring enterprise, the means of managing risk and the capacity to make the choices needed to navigate the venture. Players as they surround the driving wheel in addressing HOCs, rely more on their professional experience, probably more than from their schooling. To manage a project, a regime requires careful and competent attention to both HOCs and MOCs and their synergy. We can refer to a regime that gives such an integrated attention to both its HOCs and MOCs as undertaking 'Complete Project Management'.

This model of Complete Project Management (Figure 5.1) has been shared with many groups and audiences of project management professionals. When asked to choose the aspect where project successes and failures are most likely to occur, the preference of these professionals has always fallen strongly on Aspect B. But significantly, the emphasis still today for aspirant project professionals is that learning objectives are essentially defined to meet the competences as defined in Aspect A (MOCs). There appears to be a continuing project here for a re-think of professional and institutional priorities. The development of project professionals to become able practitioners of Complete Project Management needs to work from a fresh vision. The direction of a project is driven, or not driven, by the players and their organisation, which will always acquire a way of its own. The observations by Professor Peter Morris from the introduction are repeated here:

> *Projects, ultimately, are managed by people. Not systems, not contracts*
> *– people. People working in organisations, doing jobs, operating systems,*
> *preparing plans, making decisions, communicating (Morris, 1994: 303).*

There is a bias in many project regimes and domains, where project management tends to be regarded as the application of prescribed methods, tools and techniques – as if managing a project is a repeated or repeatable undertaking. Complete Project Management – the deployment of a combined application of HOCs and MOCs – has greater validity is a more practical formula.

Deploying Processes

Processes, formal or informal, are often key features of project management – a process being a series of actions prescribed to achieve a defined outcome. Project management is not a process. Ad hoc and temporary processes must however be continually deployed in a project, alongside more substantial, well-established, home-grown and imported processes. All provide a prescription and can be defined by what might be termed a 'script'.

The project management community has in some quarters come to regard project management itself as a process; the result of a tendency to overstate the merits of a particular management method or 'fad'. While processes are deployed to support and enable routine aspects of project management, e.g. information systems; managing a project is to sail a boat on unfamiliar waters where there will be surprises that require unexpected course corrections. Seeing a project as generally predictable is more than misleading: it denies its implicit uncertainties and complexities. All projects are unique, requiring every decision to be subject to the scrutiny of its players' resolve, observations, dialogue and organisation.

Prescribed processes to undertake routine tasks, measurement and reporting, however, have great value in their place. They can monitor progress, capture lessons learned, avoid unnecessary reinvention, deploy resources efficiently and reduce elapsed time. But there are down-sides, especially when those applying the process allow its features to distract them from the project's goals.

Every deployment of a standard process is unique and however scrupulously it might be defined, diligence will be needed to protect the quality of its application and the realisation of the outcomes intended. The defence of 'I followed procedure' when things go awry is always unacceptable and particularly alarming when expressed by someone claiming to have acted professionally. An attack of what might be termed 'Processitis', in which players allow an overdependence on process, needs to be quickly referred to the nearest Accident and Emergency Unit of the local PMO (Project Management Office).

Scepticism is an important attribute for any project management professional. It will always seek assurance that a task has been accomplished and never assume its veracity. And assurances by people and suppliers of benefits being implicit to a process have to be treated with suspicion.

'Processitis' can break out anywhere. This was demonstrated by an incident, only loosely related to project management that occurred in Haringey, London, in the summer of 2007. A young child, then referred to as 'Baby P', died as the result of parental neglect and abuse. Prior his death, local social workers assessing the child's living conditions failed to recognise the seriousness of his situation. After his death, the method of assessment that had been followed was found to have been dictated and confined by the reliance placed on a standardised process check-list. If the social workers had been more resolute in their pursuit of the actual circumstances of Baby P's case, by looking beyond the procedural discipline of the prescribed process, perhaps the child might have been rescued in time. To paraphrase a well-known aphorism, 'The price of task completion is unrelenting vigilance over the conduct of the task'.

Developing the Script

So processes are not the heart of project management. Selecting the best course of action, including the deployment of processes, must always be at the discretion of the accountable regime players. The project regime needs to be engaged in serial planning and stakeholders, including sponsors and suppliers, must be regularly involved. Moreover, the regime has to be tenacious in its attitude to risk management; to maximise the efficacy of their work and the accommodation of stakeholders' goals and preferences.

Sometimes the best that we can expect from a plan is for it to set out the purpose, the context that is envisaged; to anticipate milestones and risk; to secure resource deployment and map probable activities and stages. In navigating a project, it is the planning activity where direction is judged and where the players who live the experience sense the pace of progress, anticipate critical events and make informed choices.

A Process Iterated

It is important to recognise that project work differs from line-of-business work in the way that tasks and schedules are subjected to changes. A project has to accommodate changes through careful adaptation. Through the iteration of decisions as to what is to be achieved and how, choices need to be made that can then navigate refinement to the project's pace of progress.

In software development projects, the 'Agile Method' (Appelo, 2011) recognises that a project is largely dependent on the players' learning and re-learning. Planning here is important, but this is regular rather than far-sighted in its detail. Agile methods harvest this learning through short-interval work periods ('sprints') sometimes lasting (in software development) as little as 24 hours, at the end of which another iteration is devised on the basis of what was learned from the experience of the last sprint and what is expected of the next.

Managing projects outside the software development arena presents different challenges; sometimes with long iterations driven from a wider range of regime and contingent issues. These include adjusting to new resource constraints, design changes, change control, configuration management, new stakeholder preferences, revised requirements and remaining in alignment with a programme portfolio. Outside software development, agile methods have been deployed very effectively in new vehicle development in Japan and elsewhere.

Professional Pointers

- The abilities lying in the arenas of HOCs and MOCs need to be applied together and with rigour. They constitute a Complete Project Management capability.

- Project work needs the attention of mature project professionals and players working from a shared community.

- Developing Complete Project Management needs to work from a fresh vision of a regime's purpose and capability.

- Project management is not a process.

- Scepticism is an important attribute.

- All projects are unique, requiring every decision to be subjected to the scrutiny of its players' resolve, observations, dialogue and organisation.

- 'Processitis' can break out anywhere.

- The price of task completion is unrelenting vigilance over the conduct of the work.

References

Appelo, J. (2011). *Management 3.0.* Boston, MA: Pearson Education.

Denning, S. (2010). *Radical Management.* San Francisco, CA: Jossey-Bass.

Family Justice Council (n.d.). *Re Baby P.* Available at: http://www.judiciary. gov.uk/JCO%2FDocuments%2FFJC%2FPublications%2FBaby+P.pdf

Morris, P.W.G. (1994). *The Management of Projects.* London: Thomas Telford.

Chapter 6

A Project's Pace of Progress

*Maximising Both the Quality
and Swiftness of Delivery*

Through collective intention; balancing the goals for urgency and diligence.

Refer to the Nine Crucial Capabilities

Introduction

Projects today are deployed to meet a variety of objectives. In a rapidly changing world with its many challenges and opportunities, the need for capable project management continues to grow and diversify. Projects are deployed to deliver information systems, humanitarian interventions, engineered products, public administration, feasibility studies, drugs, defence capability, organisation change and many others.

Because of this wide range of application, every one having its particular context, standard methodologies and prescriptions applied alone, will be found to be deficient. A project's shaping, methods and path of progress have to be locally devised to suit the requirement, context, culture and domain. A project is always a unique endeavour. However the 'Pace Perspective' as explained below, applies equally to all projects. It provides a universal and comprehensive ongoing performance measure for managing the conduct of any project.

The Pace Perspective is an expedient, that gives particular attention to the key performance goals of urgency and diligence and provides a method to secure and grow the value of a project as an enterprise. Applied throughout a project life-cycle, it provides a project regime with a robust way to scrutinise its progress, intentions, ideas, priorities and decision-making. Achieving a strong pace of progress is a feature of all successful projects and this book seeks to make this more explicit and accessible to practitioners.

The Pace Perspective is a primary theme of this book. It provides new insights into project management behaviour that enhances both personal and organisational capability. It reduces dependence on 'education by trip-wire', a learning method that alas, is an all too common experience for both for projects and their practitioners.

The Pace Perspective: What Is It?

In the world of athletics, runners know that to have a chance of winning they must 'find their pace'. In medium-distance track events, judging a runner's pace is critical. For instance in the early stages of a race, if athletes run too quickly they will, as they approach the finish line, find themselves short of energy reserves. Fatigue can make it tough in the finishing sprint.

To maximise their pace of progress, runners must plan to conserve their energy by moderating their speed in the early stages of the race. They must pace their efforts, conserving energy to perform at later stages. These choices offer no certainty of victory, but they do make it more likely – offering a powerful strategy for improving the chances of winning.

Like athletes, project management practitioners, in judging their pace of progress, need to continually assess their use of time and energy as well as the quality of their work. But there are very many more factors that govern the pace of a project's progress. Project players face an abundance of choices, for example:

- The methods to adopt.

- What is possible.

- Who to persuade and how.

- What actions to scrutinise.

- When and how to engage with the customer.

- When escalation is appropriate.

- How to deploy resources.

- What to plan for.

- What estimates to accept.

- Whether to rework tasks or activities.

- When closer scrutiny is needed.

What is chosen to do and how to do it largely sets a project's pace of progress: addressing the need for both diligence and urgency and to assure the accumulation of value.

The impact of players' choices cannot be known with any certainty at the time they are made, as every choice will in some way impact on the others and be subject to circumstances that cannot be foreseen. However, despite these limitations it is through all their choices that regimes and their players are in the best position to maximise the pace of progress and to manage risks.

An Overriding Principle of Project Management

To maximise a project's pace of progress, the project regime has to continually set its priorities by the choices that it makes. A regime must weigh a project's urgency to achieve or to exceed a delivery date alongside the diligence required to meet or exceed the quality requirement or specification. An over-vigorous pursuit of one of these can easily inhibit or prevent the chances of success in the other.

For instance: inadequate scrutiny of quality can result in re-work; haste can bring error or delay. Also, excessive time spent in planning or design can be expensive or fail as an investment; a shortfall in training and development can result in mistakes and wasted resources and weak dialogue can lose opportunities to arrive at robust decisions. Striking the right balance requires resolve, experience, skilful dialogue and single-mindedness.

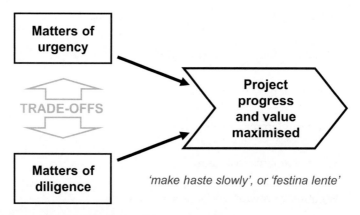

Figure 6.1   The Pace Perspective
Source: 2012 © EngagementWorks Ltd.

A regime's choices determine a project's pace of progress, its quality and reliability. Readers are invited to consider the Pace Perspective as a dominant factor determining a project's capacity to deliver on its promises (see Figure 6.1).

Maximising the pace of progress must not be confused with haste. That trap is set for players who allow themselves to be driven by naïve or inflexible scheduling. Remember the old adage 'more haste, less speed' (or the Latin *festina lente*). While the project requirement, its anticipated time-line, its quality of deliverable and budget can all constrain the pace of progress; in combination they also offer choices of more progressive routes.

Let us not pretend that we can move faster by simply proclaiming that we will do so. Progress and reliability are the result of the resolve, experience and acumen invested by players in their observations, thinking, social engagement, decision-making and collaboration.

The urgency for meeting deadlines is usually important, but so also is scrutiny, resolve, dialogue and organisation. Making well-informed choices provides us with our best chance to deploy the assets of a project management strategy, its social capital and technical expertise to best effect.

The ranges of behaviours that constitute a regime's social capital (the capability enabled by personal and social behaviour) are limitless but they are moderated and commanded by a regime's resolve, dialogue and organisation. Together, these call for the behaviours of social engagement, decision-making, devolved responsibility, reflection, assertion, humour, candour, perseverance, reasoning, community maturity and the building of a strong and positive reputation as professional practitioners, suppliers, sponsors and employers. The fate of a project is sensitive to the choices made at every level.

By attending to the pace of progress, energy and opportunities can be harnessed that may otherwise be left to remain latent. Players and their community must realise that they can liberate greater possibilities and realise the professional satisfaction that such scrutiny offers. In his account of BP's Andrew Field project regime in the North Sea, Bill Ebon of Brown and Root said: 'Once we realised that the historic tiers of authority, cross checking and approval were gone – that we were no longer waiting for permission – we grasped this freedom with relish' (see Chapter 9).

Managing the Pace of Progress

How do we know how well a project is making progress? The Pace Perspective is an inescapable and critical feature of the way that a project is managed. Its strength can be gauged from an assessment of the extent to which:

- Expectations for urgency are met – i.e. how satisfied are stakeholders that the project will achieve milestones, gateways or target dates?

- The quality of deliverables is met – i.e. how satisfied are the stakeholders that outcomes match their requirements?

- Expectations for adding value are met – i.e. how effectively is the project progressing?

To manage the pace of progress the requirements for urgency and diligence must be clearly understood and agreed. If the regime has the capacity to rise and adapt to these challenges, a strong pace of progress and a growth in value become available. Here a project manager has particular responsibility and should be a principal figure in 'stepping up to the plate'. Let's take a closer look at requirements, responses and a project manager's leadership in the pursuit of urgency and diligence (A, B and C below).

A   REQUIREMENTS OF THE STAKEHOLDERS

How should project players position themselves to sense, define and manage the stakeholder's aspirations for urgency and diligence? They can only accomplish this through their engagement with the customer, the internal sponsors and other stakeholders.

Stakeholder's expectations for urgency and diligence are often unclear or ambiguous. They commonly amount only to opinions or views. They often need to be re-stated with greater clarity – quantified as goals. An injection of project management realism and objective decision-making is usually needed. A project regime has to manage the tendency of some stakeholders to hedge their bets.

A project management professional must be proficient and persistent in achieving clarity and seeking reconciliation of the disparate requirements of all interested parties (see Chapter 4, 'Connections'). The project manager must be ready to exercise this important and complex responsibility. Procrastination and delay can seriously undermine the venture.

B   RESPONSES FROM THE PROJECT REGIME

Whatever the requirements for urgency and diligence are, how capable is a project regime in responding to them?

The qualities of responses rely on the maturity of a project regime and its behaviour as a community. The desire for both urgency and diligence has to be moderated also by a project's resource constraints and its shaping. A regime has to share continual dialogue with the customer, the internal sponsors and other stakeholders to comprehend and negotiate the requirements of stakeholders.

A project regime must seek pace through its single-mindedness, tactics, metrics, social interaction, engagement and negotiation. A 'complete' approach to project management is important (see Chapter 5).

C   LEADING THE PACE OF PROGRESS

How should a project manager and the regime of players address stakeholders' competing and conflicting attention to urgency and diligence?

Shaping a project in its early stages is important (see Chapter 1). Players must be especially alert to comprehend what is to be done, how it is to be done and their decision-making. Trade-offs pursued by particular stakeholders, as well as between them, will sustain the pace of progress. These must often be facilitated and sometimes arbitrated (see 'Diligence of Dialogue', Chapter 4).

Through their engagement with stakeholders, players have to ensure that the Pace Perspective remains centre stage. Players will sense a reassuring tempo when decisions relating to urgency and diligence are timed and judged from priorities that are authentically understood. Achieving a strong pace of progress can have a pervasive impact on a project's stamina and progress. It is expressed and delivered through the behaviour and informed choices of project players, individually and as groups.

For example, reference is made in Chapter 1 to the Andrew Field project and to a remark made by one of the contractors when commenting on the Alliance's working practices. "Having an open dialogue with the fabricators, we discovered what they really needed from us as designers."

Project Schemas and the Conduct of Project Players

A project's pace of progress is accomplished through human and organisational endeavour that includes the deployment of project management assets of standards, methodology, tools and techniques (or 'schemas'). But as demonstrated by David Beckham and Andy Murray, winning is not achieved from behaviour that has been prescribed. In managing a project, compliance with rules and standards can never be enough.

Some readers will be familiar with formulae that can be applied to the more strategic aspects of managing projects. The Theory of Constraints (TOC, Goldratt) focuses attention on a project's planning, resourcing and scheduling. The principle of Triple Constraints (Martin Barnes) recommends a set of goals (quality, cost and delivery) that test project success, targeted at the point of delivery.

The Pace Perspective centres on single-mindedness as described in this book, embracing connection, collective intention, community maturity, engagement, collaboration, critical choices and partnering with the host. It recognises that the success of a project is the result of each and every choice that is made. Choices have to be made while aware, as far as is possible, of the urgency required (the desire for swiftness) and the kind and degree of diligence required (the desire for quality).

The Roots of the Pace Perspective

The vigour of a growing plant is sustained by the capacity and health of its roots and its supply of light, water and nutrients. Below, we examine in detail critical aspects of the root system that provides, sustains and enhances a project's pace of progress.

The commonly voiced plea for 'better communication' can sometimes fail to reflect a project regime's wide-ranging dependence on rational and rigorous connections and dialogue. Exchanging information is essential to 'doing things right'. But a project regime must also respond in a collective way to emergent issues, ideas, new requirements, the players' reflections and the pace of progress. Success depends on the spirited reasoning that results from rich and informed dialogue and arguments that derive from a regime's legacy of transactions to choose both 'the right things to do' and how 'to do it right' (see Figure 5.1). Such reasoning needs to harness the players' diversity of perspective through dialogue, their engagement capability and single-mindedness.

In a line-of-business organisation, a management hierarchy is relied upon to assign roles and responsibilities to provide a framework for communication, co-ordination and control. But such a facility cannot always be relied upon in the conduct of a project. A manager's authority, roles and working relationships evolve and adapt, while its formalities will have a looser grip, circumstances becoming transitional, irregular and situation-dependent. Leadership has to be expected from all players.

In a project organisation, roles and responsibilities must adapt to revised plans, events, short-term goals, evolving circumstances, ambiguities and practicalities. The need for dialogue can become immediate and urgent. The trend is for seniors to step back from control over tasks; shifting their attention to being goal-setters, facilitators, orchestrators of dialogue, scrutineers, recruiters, patrons, winners of resources, coaches and mentors.

Communication and patterns of project work have to be advanced through a different 'router': one that will ensure that activity is well suited to current circumstances, progressive and seeking to anticipate developments. Responsibilities will often accrue to players without formal assignment; with groups forming and re-forming in their response to emergent situations as well as to comply with portfolios, strategies and plans. The project players must respond to the needs of others, as they find them.

In coping with a project's inevitable disorderliness, disciplines need to be applied more adaptably than as deployed in a line-of-business organisation. An approach to this is described in Chapter 4 referred to as the 'Gain Chain' (see Figure 4.1). It traces the pattern of a regime's progression and communication from player's sensing and thinking, through their interaction and social engagement, as the essential precursors to the effective collaboration between groups.

Players in their interactions and engagement in productive dialogue need to be emotionally mature, articulate, informed, experienced, rigorous and determined. A group's Engagement Capability enables players to harness the combined abilities of players, helping them then to act in concert through the realisation of social engagement goals (see Chapter 4). This should then provide the foundations for collaboration throughout the project regime.

Conversation helps players to open their own minds as well as those of others to uncover, scrutinise and elaborate on possibilities, options and priorities. Players as members of a professional community can then expect more reliable progress. They should also experience greater professional satisfaction from the stimulus of social interaction and from their organisation being able to afford progressive patterns of career development.

Project planning needs to be conducted from a best possible understanding of current circumstances and in anticipation of how the project is most likely seen to develop. A project is an expedition in which there will be both unexpected constraints and opportunities prompting adaptation. Continual re-planning is implicit to managing a project and its readiness depends on an early warning capability, responsiveness, well-judged decision-making and the capacity to mobilise corrective actions (see the 'Tacking Cycle' in Chapter 8).

Achieving Collective Intention

In Chapter 4, 'Connections', we considered a small and nascent motor manufacturer in Japan in the mid-1950s that had high hopes of becoming the world's most successful car maker. Their collective intention led Toyota to sell more cars than any other manufacturer by January 2013.

Collective Intention was also demonstrated by Samsung in its rise to become the largest producer of mobile phones, semiconductor memory and TV screens (see Chapter 3).

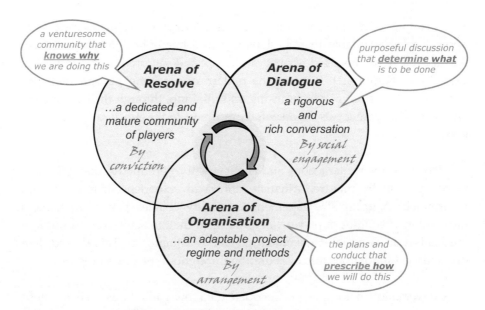

Figure 6.2   Achieving Collective Intention
Source: 2012 © EngagementWorks Ltd.

Informed choices are needed to deploy the vital assets of a regime's social and technical capital to the best effect. Three Arenas of Informed Choice addressing Resolve, Dialogue and Organisation are regularly referred in this book and address:

- *Why* we are conducting a project (a conviction);

- *What* is to be done (a conversation); and

- *How* we will do this (an organisation)

    … where the pace of progress is managed – and these are shown in Figure 6.2 above.

A project regime exercises its choices and invests its endeavours in these arenas in achieving its collective intention. The arenas are:

- The *Resolve Arena* … calling for Conviction – where a project regime determines *why* this will be done.

- The *Dialogue Arena* ... calling for Social Engagement and Collaboration – where a project regime determines *what* is to be done.

- The *Organisation Arena* ... calling for effective Arrangements – where a project regime determines *how* it will be done.

Attention to any one of these arenas in the absence of the other two is unlikely to have a favourable impact on progress. It is only through the synergies between the three that the strongest progress is possible.

A project regime has to continually make choices. On each and every occasion the three arenas must be visited and the requirements for urgency and diligence assessed. Through these considerations the choices made by the regime's players, singly and in groups, can most effectively decide the most progressive path. Aside from externally imposed events, the combined impact of all a regime's choices. determine the paths to be followed and the pace of progress.

A project's trajectory and pace of progress is critical to project success. The quality of decision-making relies on the sensing, experience and judgement of the regime's players; the efficacy of their working practices and their handling of personal, ethical and strategic issues. In *Managing Business Ethics*, Linda K. Treviño and Katherine A. Nelson say that:

> business isn't just better when companies and business people are ethical, but rather that good ethics is absolutely essential *for effective business practice. This is not just empty rhetoric. Work is essential to life and most people work for a business of some kind. How we work and the standards that we uphold while we are working, affect more than just commerce. Our business behaviour also affects our personal and company reputations, politics, society at large and even our national reputation (Treviño and Nelson, 2011: 3–4; emphasis original).*

Making choices navigates a project's progress. And when making their choices regimes need to be able to accommodate controversy through their observation, imagining, reasoning, tolerance and social engagement.

Table 6.1 provides examples of behaviours that serve Resolve, Dialogue and Organisation as these are conducted in the management of a project. They are listed in no particular order and some occur to more than one arena. This table perhaps demonstrates the crucial importance of players' behaviour in the conduct of a project.

Table 6.1   Behaviours in the Arenas of Informed Choice: Choosing the Path and Setting the Pace of Progress

Arena of Resolve: A dedicated and mature community of players	Arena of Dialogue: A rigorous and rich conversation	Arena of Organisation: An adaptable project regime and methods
• Ensure alignment with the portfolio • Drive through short-interval goals • Promote high, realistic expectations • Make persistence a virtue • Sustain resolute leadership • Agree the requirement, continually • Engage with customers and users • Maximise the pace of progress • Claim the value zone • Mediate to reconcile disagreement • Persist with rapid follow-up of issues • Disallow unnecessary delay • Liaise with dependent functions • Track the costs of engagement • Manage tacking (course redirection) • Avoid or resolve political hurdles • Make leadership pervasive • Follow up decisions promptly • Maintain order within disorder • Harness community energies	• Share news throughout the regime • Reaffirm purpose and requirement • Engage to enrich ideas and options • Collaborate for action and outcomes • Engage closely with stakeholders • Strengthen groups as 'safe places' • Mentor players for their leadership and development (L and D) • Review task priorities, continually • Sustain a community of practice • Uphold values and intentions • Brainstorm ideas and solutions • Listen to and harness diversity • Scrutinise ideas and project Issues • Inspire the regime and its vision • Recognise players' contributions • Celebrate achievement • Foster social interaction • Foster conversational skill • Foster productive argument • Discourage hesitation	• Value campaigns over skirmishes • Assign and clarify responsibilities • Accommodate all stakeholders • Target the triple constraints • Hold players accountable • Settle personal issues • Resolve political issues • Connect autonomous endeavours • Deploy standards and methods • Require competence and courtesy • Recruit and retain talent • Build orderliness and morale • Promote loose–tight behaviours • Make Learning and Development implicit goals • Recognise merit • Promote community ethos • Be equipped and ready to adapt • Expect and recognise leadership • Measure progress and respond • Log events and transactions

Source: 2012 © EngagementWorks Ltd.

Tables 6.2, 6.3 and 6.4 illustrate the importance of the choices made by players and their regimes. Some samples of choices encountered by players are listed under their Arena headings. They together reveal many of the issues that underpin the strength of a project regime and illustrate the impact of them in short and long-term time-frames. These examples give attention to customer relations; self-image and reputation; professional visibility; consistency of behaviour; confronting or avoiding issues; questioning or assuming the requirement; checking for task completion; saying what needs to be said.

Table 6.2   Resolve Arena – Some Choices

	Choice	A challenging option within this choice
R1	Assume alignment with the portfolio *or* ensure that there is alignment	... insist on implementation of the strategy
R2	Challenge the argument *or* roll-over the argument	... put a project's purpose ahead of the risk of losing face
R3	Serve the case for short-term *or* serve the case for long-term	... go for the option that builds maturity
R4	Win colleagues' favour *or* insist on discipline	... put aside the pursuit of popularity ... sustain ethos and standards and win respect
R5	Argue to refute ideas *or* argue to explore ideas	... know your argument: seek value and purpose
R6	Accept the sponsor's wishes *or* question their wishes	... press your argument and resolve through social engagement
R7	Regularly interrogate the requirement *or* assume requirement to be unchanged	...continually verify and confirm project requirements
R8	Step out from the crowd *or* hide inside the crowd	... accept responsibility to act professionally
R9	Capability of the enterprise first *or* customer first	... check out capability before making promises
R10	Support the group's endeavours *or* pursue your own interests	... place the project's interests ahead of personal interests

Source: 2012 © EngagementWorks Ltd.

Table 6.3   Dialogue Arena – Some Choices

	Choice	A challenging option within this choice
D1	Simply receive information, no question *or* ensure your understanding of it	... accumulate comprehension through persistent curiosity
D2	Interrogate to gather information *or* conduct appreciative inquiry	... converse, develop a relationship to uncover the reality

Table 6.3   Continued

	Choice	A challenging option within this choice
D3	Reveal your feelings to others *or* hide your feelings from others	… find low-risk behaviours to enable candour
D4	Offer eager compliance *or* exercise intelligent disobedience	… find the best way to promote your own convictions
D5	Seek harmony though silence *or* seek progress through openness	… find a way to say what you know needs to be said
D6	Anticipate crucial conversation *or* prefer to converse spontaneously	… recognise that dialogue is often crucial
D7	Conduct dialogue in order to learn *or* conduct dialogue to get action	… make the purpose of discourse explicit
D8	Say what you believe to be true *or* say what you see to be expedient	… recognise that issues need to be confronted
D9	Sustain the 'safe place' in meetings *or* allow disclosure of proceedings	… when necessary, confine knowledge to the group
D10	Use an open and empathetic approach *or* be sceptical and searching	… favour appreciative enquiry over explicit scrutiny

Source: 2012 © EngagementWorks Ltd.

Table 6.4   Organisation Arena – Some Choices

	Choice	A challenging option within this choice
O1	Take a process outcome to be 'as read' *or* authenticate every outcome	… judge carefully the necessity for validation
O2	Formalise your authority *or* win your reputation and status	… work with diligence to secure trusting relationships
O3	Use published templates *or* devise customised methods	… resist blind compliance to process
O4	Partner with a sponsor *or* accept direction from a sponsor	… in discourse, act upon your judgements
O5	Follow the 'corporate way' *or* insist on a 'project way'	… avoid business routines unsuited to PM practices
O6	Deploy standard operating procedures (SOPs)/ standards/policies *or* deviate for pragmatic reasons	… choose the course of action fit for purpose
O7	Make decisions instinctively *or* act only following analysis	… when necessary, insist on thorough scrutiny
O8	Purge deviances *or* normalise deviances	… listen actively to emergent ideas and practices
O9	Scrutinise plans and intentions *or* 'give the nod'	… be suspicious of a clamour for an urgent decision
O10	Allow loose planning *or* ensure that plans are specific	… always resist 'fact-free' planning

Source: 2012 © EngagementWorks Ltd.

The Social Experience, Behaviour and Leadership

The key to successful leadership today is influence, not authority.

Ken Blanchard

In conducting the management of a project, the player's opinions, attitudes and preferences will have been influenced by their engagement with other players and by the ideas, principles and arguments encountered from other sources.

In this way the professional choices that are made by players can be affected by their observation of the behaviour of other players. Patterns of behaviour and decision-making in a project regime are developed in this way. They influence for example, relationships, social engagement, loyalties, collegiality, conformity, conflict avoidance, conflict resolution, prejudices, decision-making, skepticism, disapproval, leadership and the capacity for dialogue. In 1958, Harvard psychologist, Herbert Kelman (Kelman, 1958) identified three broad kinds of social influence:

1.   Compliance is when people appear to agree with others, but actually keep their dissenting opinions private.

2.   Identification is when people are influenced by someone who is liked and respected, such as a famous celebrity.

3.   Internalization is when people accept a belief or behavior and agree it both publicly and privately.

Some behaviours in an organisation when adopted in this way, become 'normalised' as 'the way that we do things around here'. They sometimes become cultural protocols that may then be allowed to mature as practices that have become preferred. They then can be regarded as an asset to a regime, but they can also frustrate working arrangements, adaptation, innovation and attempts to improve professional practices.

Leadership in a project community will often use familiar cultural protocols to compare and contrast ideas. Project players need to be persistent in their exploitation of both regularly used and novel protocols to judge their value and to fashion and re-fashion their use in dialogue and productive arguments on which decision-making depends.

Examples of cultural protocols include:

- 'We recognise that our success is attributable to our curiosity and persistent learning'.

- 'The opinions of everyone in the community must be respected and heard'.

- 'Senior players make the decisions; other players amount to the project resource'.

- 'Regular and active dialogue and conversation is a critical activity'.

- 'All critical assumptions, calculations and arguments must be recorded'.

- 'Achieving short-term benefits' is our first and primary priority'.

- 'Our project managers must have grown-up in this industry'.

- 'Interest in the views and concerns of customers is paramount'.

- 'Interest in the profitability of a contract is paramount'.

- 'All design specifications must be signed-off by the Head of Design'.

- 'The continuous improvement to products and capability is everyone's responsibility'.

Professional Pointers

- Standard project management principles and practices, if applied alone, would be inadequate.

- If athletes run too quickly in the early stages of a race, they will, as they approach the finishing line, find themselves short of energy reserves.

- Decisions relating to urgency and diligence have to be timed and judged from priorities that are well defined and understood What is chosen to do and how to do it largely sets a project's pace of progress.

- An over-vigorous pursuit of one of these can easily inhibit or prevent the chances of triumph in the otherIn managing a project, compliance with rules and standards can never be enough.

- A project manager has particular responsibility as a principal figure, to 'step up to the plate'.

- For a project to navigate its progress successfully, the Gain Chain has to be pursued with rigour.

- Players will sense a reassuring tempo to their progress when decisions relating to urgency and diligence are judged from priorities that are well defined and understood.

- Compliance with rules and standards cannot ever be enough.

Reference

Treviño, L.K. and Nelson, K.A. (2011). *Managing Business Ethics: Straight Talk about How to Do It Right*. Hoboken, NJ: Wiley.

PART III
Assuring Success

Chapter 7

A Project's Persistence

Achieving Constancy, Despite Constraints and the Social/Political Mood

> Ensuring that purpose, pace and progress meet with challenges and setbacks.
>
> *Refer to the Nine Crucial Capabilities*

Introduction

To prosper, a project has to resolve the issues and questions that challenge its goals, the methods that it uses and the impact that they have on the pace of progress. Arriving at decisions, implementing those decisions and defending them will always test the capability and endurance of a project regime – but it is persistence that correlates with reliability. (These features of persistence are demonstrated in the accounts of resolute leadership exemplified by the work of Lee Kun-hee (Samsung), Sir Richard Branson (Virgin), Sir Ralph Robins (Rolls-Royce) and Steve Jobs (Apple Inc.) (see Chapter 3).

Persistence in sustaining the progress of a high-risk project can become the most demanding aspect of managing a project, as well as having an impact on its credibility. Also, social psychology as revealed in the work Festinger, Milgram, Zimbardo and others, have helped us to understand ways in which others in society can have a profound influence on our thinking and behaviour. Project professionals should be aware of these effects (for example, cognitive dissonance, compliance under authority, group think and perception) and be prepared to identify and judge such behaviours when adverse to player's conduct. While the persistence of a project regime may be apparent from its constancy of purpose, execution and progress, these qualities are ultimately attributable to the conduct of the project players themselves.

Perhaps the most thoroughly surveyed sector of project management performance is the IT sector. A prominent research company is the Standish Group and in 2013 it reported a marginal increase in PM success or 'project resolution rates'. This report attributes performance to project management 'processes, methods, skills, costs, tools, decisions, optimisation, internal and external influences and team chemistry'. The majority of the projects surveyed were reported to have either 'failed' or were 'challenged' (Table 7.1). We can only speculate as to how the difficulties experienced in these projects were caused by or languished from weaknesses of persistence.

	2004	2006	2008	2010	2012
Successful	19%	35%	32%	37%	39%
Failed	18%	19%	24%	21%	18%
Challenged	53%	48%	44%	42%	43%

Table 7.1   'Think Big, Act Small'
Source: The Standish Group (2013), *CHAOS Manifesto 2013: Think Big, Act Small*.

Accounts of persistence and its beneficial effects are more commonly reported than instances of project management deficiencies. But criticism of a professional player or group of players on these grounds will often point to some personal weakness of players; risking resentment on their part. This should not, however, be allowed to inhibit such a concern being shared between players and their mentor, functional manager or sponsor. It is perhaps why persistence as a factor of project management performance does not appear in The Standish Group's list above.

This chapter seeks to explore the meaning and significance of persistence as a factor in the management of projects. It explores examples of persistent conduct; instances of where such behaviour is positive, disruptive or lacking in its consequences. The complexity and uncertainties of some projects themselves will remain intractable without the concerted and persistent endeavour of players (see Chapter 4, 'Diligence of Dialogue'). Recent studies and research in this arena are explained and explored.

A Crucial Factor Difficult to Define

Three stories follow to illustrate the impact of persistence in the management of projects.

STORY ONE

This concerns an advanced and complex project undertaken by a British defence contractor. On a notable occasion, the contractor's senior managers expressed concern about the project's progress. A review meeting was called at which the customer shared their concern. In his response, the project manager explained that he would continue to follow the plan that he had devised and had shown them. He said that he had no reason to change it and suggested that he proceed with it unless the company or its customer requested his resignation. They did not do so, and his persistence on the matter led to the project's success. For some years following, customers would specifically request that this person manage the project that they wished to commission.

Persistence here featured strongly in sustaining the implementation of a complex project. It was born of the confidence, reputation and courage of an able project manager. The story also illustrates how observers of a project regime, albeit as a sponsor or customer, must in some cases accept that their appreciation and understanding of the forces at work in a project may be limited.

STORY TWO

Robert Noyce and Gordon Moore founded Intel in 1968 when they left Fairchild Semiconductor. Intel became a leading designer and fabricator of microchips and was responsible for the introduction of the microprocessor. Arthur Rock, the chairman of Intel's board and a major investor in the company, said that for Intel to succeed they needed Noyce, Moore and Grove – in that order. He explained that Noyce, the visionary, was born to inspire; Moore was the virtuoso of technology; and Grove was the technologist turned management scientist.

The relaxed culture that Noyce brought to Intel was a carry-over from the style that he developed at Fairchild Semiconductor. He treated employees as family, rewarding and encouraging teamwork. His 'follow your bliss' management style set the tone for many Silicon Valley success stories. Noyce's management style was also called a 'roll up your sleeves' style. He shunned exotic corporate cars, reserved parking spaces, private jets, plush offices and furnishings in favour of a less structured, relaxed working environment in which all had high expectations of one another. No one received lavish benefits. By declining the usual executive perks he stood as a model for future generations of Intel CEOs. Robert Noyce's persistence in creating and sustaining an open and collaborative style led to him being labelled the 'Mayor of Silicon Valley'.

Persistence by Robert Noyce was shown by his part in growing a business enterprise and culture that has dominated the industry. It served as a catalyst in the development of the global semiconductor industry that in 2013 exceeding $23 billion in sales. From its beginning, Noyce persisted in the implementation of a rigorous and energetic work culture that heralded the development of new technologies, a shrewd management style and a dynamic organisation.

STORY THREE

The stunningly majestic cathedral of Orvieto is located in central Italy (Figure 7.1). Pope Urban IV commissioned the cathedral to celebrate the Miracle of Bolsena in 1263. It took 30 years to plan and three centuries to build. Over many generations, a succession of architects, builders, artists and sculptors collaborated to produce one of the artistic masterpieces of the Italian Middle Ages. Of course the majority of them did not see the finished product, or could have hoped to do so. The persistence of these creators and of course its sponsor the church, is difficult to comprehend in the modern age, but nevertheless the story persists as a lesson. There was in the thirteenth century evidently great pride and competition between the Italian states engaged in the construction of their religious buildings.

Persistence in building the cathedral at Orvieto was shown by sponsors who nurtured and supported the design and construction of a magnificent building, bringing great prestige to the town of Orvieto and to the Church as an institution. Persistence over 300 years by successive architects, builders, artists and craftsmen enabled a project that succeeded in its resolve over a very long period of time, with a dialogue and an organisation able to produce an artefact of the highest standard.

These three stories illustrate the significance of persistence in the management of a project. In Story One the project manager's persistence served to sustain the confidence of the defence equipment supplier and its customer when the details of a complex project were not and could not be fully comprehended by its principal stakeholders. In Story Two a business leader was able to persistently promote the value of a work culture conducive to scientific and engineering innovation, resulting in the emergence of a

Figure 7.1   The Cathedral at Orvieto, Italy
Source: © The author.

substantial new business enterprise and industry. Through the persistence of Noyce, these innovative working practices became widely adopted. In Story Three the persistence of town councillors and a pervasive and a powerful Church regime, sustained a project that was able to endure in its constancy over an extraordinarily long period, and far longer than any of its protagonists.

Persistence of a Single-Minded Project Management Regime

Persistence is a powerful source of vitality that can bring higher levels of energy to a project's endeavours. It is a particularly powerful force when mobilised by a group of people sharing a common determination. The three arms of Collective Intention (see Chapter 4) are used below to illustrate some of the behaviours of a project regime able to perform persistently and single-mindedly.

I   RESOLVE AND TENACITY

1.   The sponsor's purpose and values are continually stated.

2.   The regime's choices are made to maximise the pace of progress.

3.   Leadership is expected of all players supporting and sustaining the endeavour.

4.   Successes are openly recognised and reported.

5.   Favourable behaviour is encouraged through the example of seniors.

6.   Errors and mistakes serve as sources of learning and development.

2   DIALOGUE AND CONNECTION

1.   What needs to be said, finds a way to be said.

2.   Players behave in a way that is emotionally mature.

3.   Social interaction enables dialogue; yielding connections and new ideas.

4.   Groups rely on rich and relevant social engagement enabling collaboration.

5.   Players widely consult and involve others to enable connections.

6.   Shared purpose and commitment help to accommodate differences.

3   ORGANISATION AND ADAPTATION

1.   Roles and responsibilities are widely understood and seen to evolve.

2.   Projects depend on the pursuit of enterprise by all players.

3.   Players distinguish matters substantial from matters circumstantial.

4.   Professional standards of conduct are expected.

5.   People's learning and development are primary regime goals.

6.   The project regime retains a level of autonomy.

Persistence and the 'Paradigm Paradox'

In conducting a major project, players have to find ways to be concerted and to act with persistence. They must exert themselves to a level of professional and organisational agility rarely expected elsewhere in public or commercial life.

Despite the scale of a project, its complexity and uncertainties, players need to stretch themselves to think productively; always engaging together to devise plans for innovation and collaboration. And today all organisations are experiencing a degree of 'projectisation'. As Tom Taylor, president of the APM, has said: 'Most people are now involved in the work of one or more project; full time, part-time or sometime'.

Darren Dalcher, now Professor of Project Management at the University of Hertfordshire, said at the APM conference in 2010: 'Ours is a world that demands what appears to be the impossible. The challenge for the profession is to develop its future'.

The situation is not one confined only to those who see themselves as project management professionals. It is the predicament of all sectors where there is a determination to advance performance and the pace of progress. Organisations have to continually renew themselves and their organisation to operate and trade competitively; changing the way that they behave and function to match prevailing and anticipated conditions.

While there is no shortage of research describing the practical difficulties of managing projects, many experienced project managers see there to be a primary root cause of success and failure. They consistently report a contradiction that can be referred to as the 'paradigm paradox'. Its victims are trapped in an obsolete world in which doctrines that sustain outdated attitudes, role inflexibility and process rigidity too often prevail.

Some senior managers, while commonly attributing weaknesses in capacity and performance to deficiencies in professional competence and organisation, nevertheless hesitate to implement remedial measures. Commonly, they attribute limitations to 'the culture'; arguing this to be the root cause. The habits of players' behaviour, however inappropriate are seen by many to be too deep-rooted to permit the necessary changes to behaviour. Their claim is that 'their people' are either too unwilling or unable to adapt. The issue is then banished to the 'too hard tray' (lying between the 'in' and 'out' trays). Many who suffer this paradox are even reluctant to recognise the crucial differences that distinguish an organisation intended for business as usual from one that as a project, is required to persistently adapt.

A Failure of Professional Persistence

The space shuttle *Challenger* exploded shortly after lift-off on 28 January 1986. The launch had been scheduled for 22 January. It was delayed until the 28 January following a series of problems. The NASA managers, feeling the pressure from Congress, became particularly eager to get the mission underway. On the 27th an engineer signalled a 'red flag', referring to concerns he and others had regarding the O-rings in the booster rockets. Several conference calls were held to discuss the issue before NASA's decision to go ahead with the launch. The O-ring failure was, in the subsequent enquiry, seen by some to be the cause of the disaster. The Presidential Commission, however, reported the root cause to be human failure in NASA's organisation.

It concluded that weaknesses in NASA's organisational culture and decision-making processes had been the key contributing factors causing the accident. Managers had failed to adequately communicate to senior officials the engineers' growing doubts about the seal. The unrelenting pressure to meet the demands of an accelerated flight schedule had resulted in them compromising vital safety and quality standards and procedures. The organisation lacked the necessary persistence.

Under this political pressure NASA had contradicted the goals that they had set themselves. The official enquiry also cited the team's feeling of invulnerability, the pressure from Congress and the 'groupthink' pattern of social conformity in which they failed to properly examine the risks attaching to their decisions.

In *Challenger Launch Decision* (Vaughan, 1996), Diane Vaughan examines not only the parts played by NASA engineers and managers, but also the behaviour of members of the Presidential Commission. She uses the term 'normalised deviance' to describe how NASA's managers misrepresented data to align with and endorse a corporate purpose. The behaviour became habituated and was unchallenged.

Vaughan also describes the contribution from one of the Commissioners: Richard Feynman, a scientist and Nobel prize-winner renowned for his objectivity, persistence and ability to present complex ideas simply. He was the only independent member of the Commission – the rest representing interested parties. At a public hearing of the Commission, Feynman demonstrated that the rubber O-ring material on the day of the launch lost its resiliency at low temperatures. He did this to the surprise of the hearing, demonstrating the issue on live national television. Using a sample from the rubber O-ring and his glass of iced water provided for refreshment, he was able, very simply, to refute NASA's claim of the rubber's robust physical properties at low temperature.

His interjection enabled the re-evaluation of the Commission's understanding of the accident. Their findings had more to say about NASA's behaviour and organisation than it did about its technology and work processes.

Feynman's behaviour at the hearing was a vivid example of the skill and courage often needed from a member of a group when engaged together in critical dialogue when the stakes are high. This behaviour will always be needed for breaking through groupthink, people's personal mind-sets and stand-offs that are politically motivated, or for protecting personal or other vested interests.

Sustaining Impetus and Resolve

The Nine Crucial Capabilities (see Table P.1) together represent what needs to be done to manage a project. But to assure a project's pace of progress, reliability and success, something more inspiring is often deployed to sustain a project's Impetus and Resolve. An 'overarching purpose' has sometimes to be found that lies beyond a project's formally stated objectives and to be either implicitly or explicitly promoted.

Impetus and Resolve can be seen to be drawing upon 'Compelling Forces' (see Figure 7.2) to drive a project's pace of progress. These are chosen in a way that represents the essence of why the project is being undertaken. They have to be relevant and firmly anchored to the prevailing culture, values and its aspirations. The purpose of Compelling Forces is to harness the determination of players and stakeholders to be successful and for Impetus and Resolve to be an issue that is subjected to player's regular evaluation and dialogue. Table 7.2 shows examples of projects and their overarching purpose.

Table 7.2   Strengthening Impetus and Resolve – Examples

Project	Overarching Purpose
Search and recovery of Malaysian 'plane MH370	The re-assurance of airline passengers
Building a wind farm	Moderating the damage caused by global warning
Reducing production costs and product quality	Growing market share
Establishing a school debating club	Developing able citizens

Any measure that is chosen to build and sustain 'Impetus and Resolve' needs to serve as an inspiration as well as form part of a project's rationale. The hope is of course that it will inject energy and vitality into a project venture and help to represent an enterprise that is strong and coherent. However such measures must be allowed to evolve, can be difficult to sustain and are easily compromised.

'Impetus and Resolve' is described in Figure 7.2 under three headings:

- Clear Mission – cogent reasons to undertake a project.

- Compelling Forces – factors that build capability, confidence and collaboration.

- Crucial Capabilities – features of effective conduct and behaviour.

Figure 7.2   Impetus and Resolve

Source: 2012 © EngagementWorks Ltd.

Examples of projects that, to a significant extent, owe their success to 'Impetus and Resolve' and a Compelling Force include.

- *'Mulberry Harbour', the project to invade the beaches of Northern France in 1944*: The imperative here was to rapidly establish a logistical entry into hostile territory. The project required an immense planning effort and had to draw on every aspect of the allied armed forces' capability.

- *Developing the Andrew Field, an oil production platform in Britain's North Sea in 1995* (see page 15): The 'compelling forces' here were the pursuit of cost-reduction and proving the application of Alliance Working to replace traditional contract working practices in the North Sea (see Chapter 1).

- *Developing high density semiconductor memory components by Samsung in the 1990s*: Through its persistence and enterprise, Samsung developed the first 64Mb, 256Mb and 1Gb semiconductor DRAMs effectively eliminating competition in this mass volume market

- *Replacing sections of a main railway line on the UK south coast that were destroyed by a sea storm in the winter of 2014*: An urgent project in which 300 workers with their single-mindedness and professionalism, re-built the cliffs, a new sea wall, station platform and laid new tracks over a period of just 6 weeks while regularly battered by further heavy storms.

- *Clearing nuclear contaminated land at Rocky Flats Colorado, USA 2007* (see page 179): A highly profitable and enterprising project cleared a large nuclear weapons site in Colorado harnessing innovation that was devolved all players, with stakeholder and workforce collaboration.

Functional Stupidity: A Denial of Professional Persistence

Functional stupidity is defined as the 'refusal to use intellectual resources outside a narrow and "safe" terrain' (Alvesson and Spicer, 2012). Examples include the US and European banks' failure to scrutinise their financial models and the behaviours that led to the financial crises of 2008. It was exhibited in the errors that led to the *Challenger* disaster and the 'normalised deviance' displayed by managers at NASA. Functional stupidity is perhaps most observable to project management professionals from the habit of discounting the need for project shaping and planning prior to initiation – prompting the dictum 'Failure to plan is planning to fail'. In the paper 'A stupidity-based theory of organizations' reference is made to:

> *A blinkered approach to organisational problems, wherein people show unwillingness to consider or think about solutions that lie outside an arbitrary boundary. A common example of this is when a group explicitly excludes certain topics or that they are tacitly deemed as being 'out of bounds' for discussion. Many 'business as usual' scenarios are riddled with functional stupidity, which is precisely why it's often so hard to detect (Alvesson and Spicer, 2012).*

Persistence in Overcoming Complexity and Disorder

A project presents its players with issues and problems that, as it proceeds, change their form and meaning as well as interact with each other. This is a challenge that takes us beyond a situation of complication into what is now known instead as 'complexity' – where problems cannot be handled in isolation from others and the possible routes to progress seem perplexing in their means of access.

A project's goals and circumstances are always unique and we can never be entirely confident of acquiring a complete understanding. However, while a project's ambiguity and complexities endure, progress has to be made, albeit that outside observers continue to report scenes of disorder.

In situations of complexity and uncertainty the culture of an organisation must have a major influence on what a project regime can expect to achieve. Its values and behaviours are likely to play a crucial part in determining a regime's capability for resolving issues. Most importantly, it needs to cultivate and sustain a capacity for adaptation and also sometimes humour; to the way it addresses a project and to its capacity as an organisation to do so.

A project regime needs the virtue of curiosity and openness to possibilities while also being decisive in the implementation of a chosen plan and method of execution. There is an approach that encourages patterns of behaviours that will accommodate such a 'loose style' to generate new and productive ideas with a corresponding 'tight style' that provides for formality and is disciplined in its endeavours. A regime needs the benefits of both; conducted in such a way that one does not consume the other. For this, players must be enabled by a 'cabaret' of endeavour, drawing together a medley of scrutiny, dialogue, imagination and pace. Tom Peters and Bob Waterman promote 'Simultaneous Loose-Tight Properties' (Peters and Waterman, 1981: Chapter 12).

Some readers will know of the work of Charles Pellerin, former Director of Astrophysics for NASA, author of *How NASA Builds Teams* (Pellerin, 2009) and his references to 'group social risk'. He recounts those occasions when a group of committed project players move into deep and meaningful conversation, and where robust debate and argument is experienced. Typically, there is energetic discussion, competitive behaviour and posturing. Insights are generated and there are frequent opportunities for both conflict and synergy. Pride and perhaps reputation are at stake and feelings rise. The occasion can be very productive, but it can also turn out to be disruptive and even damaging. Normal rules of engagement, including the pursuit of orderliness, are commonly suspended as the result of explicitly expressed feelings. There can be three kinds of outcome from such events.

1.   Amounting to a down-side risk: a quarrel in which views clash and the occasion becomes one in which there is rancour that brings fresh hazards and threats to the project.

2.   Amounting to an up-side risk: a brainstorm results in the birth of an inventive and promising idea or solution.

3.   Amounting to a 'non-event': a groupthink in which a particular theme or view of limited value is allowed to dictate proceedings.

Number 2 is obviously the preferred outcome and in many instances where creativity and/or support through consensus is at stake (and it usually is), such an event can turn out to bring significant value to a project's enterprise.

Charles Pellerin says:

> My inquiry into this generally unnoticed form of risk began 30 years ago when my friend and NASA scientist John Mather remarked, 'Charlie, I believe that half of a project's cost is socially determined'. At the time, he was referring to the Cosmic Background Explorer, the mission for which he earned a Nobel Prize in physics. Actually, I did not give this the attention it deserved until the Hubble Space Telescope's Failure Review Board named 'leadership failure' as the root cause of the flawed mirror. For the eight years preceding the failure, I was NASA's director of astrophysics and leader of the Hubble development team. This 'leadership failure' was mine. Leadership is a social ability, not a technical ability. 'Social risk' is real (Pellerin, 2009: xiv).

We have all experienced the mental stimulation of conversation and how this can rouse and enrich our thinking. The phenomenon and its potential value to social engagement are now being actively explored by academics and will always be a powerful source of strength to a project management regime.

Terry Cooke-Davies et al. (2007) describe scientific investigations into the behaviour of complex dynamic systems, reporting insights that, if valid, will have major implications for expanding the prevailing assumptions that now underpin project management practices. There are pointers here towards new ways of thinking and talking about managing complexity and managing projects in ways that may resolve the intractable problems that plague some areas of project management. The paper examines a framework for understanding the 'complex responsive processes of relating' (CRPR), referring to the ways that players interact and how these interactions serve not only the need for communication and relationships between players but also act as catalysts for learning and appreciation. Specifically, it discusses the experiences of project groups when delivering projects that involve significant complexity. It describes the way that language shapes meaning and the way that cultural paradigms shape practice. It also explains the implications of using such a paradigm to enhance project management practice.

One of the co-authors of this paper, Svetlana Cicmil, encourages practising project managers to pay attention to the qualities of the patterns of conversations and the dynamics within groups of people in the way that they relate to one another. She encourages the participation of project players in acting as leaders of dialogue and learning to live with the anxiety of players. She encourages project players to reflect upon the paradox of 'becoming' rather than 'being' in control of a project while nevertheless remaining able to sustain productive joint action. Perhaps our subconscious has a greater part to play in our actions than we are able to testify.

In summary, the work of Peters and Waterman – and later that of Pellerin, Cooke-Davies et al. and contributors to *Making Projects Critical* (Hodgson and Cicmil, 2006) – helps us to understand that behaviour between players when this can 'run free' can be an important means of coping with complexity and facilitating creativity. Project players, when conducting the process of brainstorming – and in doing so setting aside formalised process prescriptions – enter this same arena. The articulation of players' thinking that may otherwise be inhibited and lost to the enterprise can sometimes be more readily revealed in this way, enriching the possibilities for the pace of progress and a project's reliability.

Professional Pointers

*   The dependence of projects on resolute leadership.

*   Accounts of positive persistence are more common than reports of its absence.

*   The importance of confidence, reputation and courage.

*   The crucial support of a sponsor who is persistent and promotes endurance.

- Collective Intention as represented by resolution, dialogue and organisation.

- Confronting the 'paradigm paradox' and 'normalised deviance'.

- A stupidity-based theory of organisation

- Beyond a situation of complication there is the challenge of complexity.

- Simultaneous loose-tight behaviours.

- 'Nothing in this world can take the place of persistence'.

References

Alvesson, M. and Spicer, A. (2012). A stupidity-based theory of organizations. *Journal of Management Studies*, 49(7): 1194–220.

Cooke-Davies, T., Cicmil, S., Crawford, L. and Richardson, K. (2007). We're not in Kansas anymore, Toto: Mapping the strange landscape of complexity theory, and its relationship to project management. *Project Management Journal*, 38(2): 50–61.

Hodgson, D. and Cicmil, S. (2006). *Making Projects Critical*. Basingstoke: Palgrave Macmillan.

Pellerin, C.J. (2009). *How NASA Builds Teams: Mission Critical Soft Skills for Scientists, Engineers, and Project Teams*. Hoboken, NJ: Wiley.

Peters, T.J. and Waterman, R.H. (1981). *In Search of Excellence: Lessons from America's Best-Run Companies*. New York: Harper and Row.

The Standish Group (2013). *CHAOS Manifesto 2013: Think Big, Act Small*. Available at: http://versionone.com/assets/img/files/CHAOSManifesto2013.pdf [accessed 7 May 2014].

Vaughan, D. (1996). *Challenger Launch Decision: Risky Technology, Culture, and Deviance at NASA*. Chicago, IL: University of Chicago Press.

Chapter 8

The Project's Adaptation

Responding Effectively to Circumstances That Change

Acting promptly and effectively to any call for redirection, correction or rework.

Refer to the Nine Crucial Capabilities

Introduction

In deciding the best routes to make progress a project regime will wish to know the likely impact of the options available. However, the uncertainties and complexities of a project mean that the outcome of any choice is unlikely to be knowable at the time that it is decided. A project evolves from its many activity streams and their interactions. A regime must make their decisions whilst recognising this as an implicit risk.

A project is an expedition having few prescriptions on which to rely. Plans replace earlier plans; but for a regime giving close attention to its planning, its luck will grow. A project can usefully be regarded as 'a network of commitments', in which players striving to meet its interests and goals, endeavour to make the appropriate connections: usually their best assurance for maximising the pace of progress.

Project practitioners have to recognise that decisions are made within the context of current issues as they are then perceived. Choosing an action, its priority has to be based on the state of the project as it is then understood. Players need to be connected, curious, socially engaged, inventive and tenacious as well methodical and prudent with resources.

In navigating through a project's uncertainties, risk management and adaptation are principal features of its management. This chapter includes a consideration of circumstances in which a project regime is required to work with a line-of-business organisation (for example with its host organisation). It argues that very many of a project's challenges lie in a regime's own back yard but nonetheless are the result of insufficient attention given to the external environment. The limitations of a strictly systematic approach are also recognised and addressed.

Two methods are described here to help facilitate adaptation. The first introduces a way of managing 'Discovery and Redirection' by mapping the practical issues involved in executing a project's adaptation to unplanned events using what is labelled the 'Tacking Cycle'. The second provides a set of 'Adaptation Goals' for ensuring that a project regime is well prepared for upcoming events that are likely to require a project's adaptation. Collaboration software is considered at the end of the chapter.

A Regime's Adaptation to Circumstances

A project is required to meet a unique set of requirements. As it develops, plans will be continually revised and a regime will periodically review their working arrangements and methods. When circumstances impose a more serious and immediate challenge, a project regime must be ready and able to quickly adapt itself. Unexpected constraints or opportunities can change the requirement and the way in which it is to be met. Like the project itself and its management, a regime has to evolve and develop through additions and adaptations to its own capabilities.

We cannot know how a project will develop: what will transpire, what will be learned and how this will affect later decisions. Whereas a business process may be assured by regular and reliable policy and procedures, such routines are not the ways of a project's endeavour. The project's purpose, its way of working and the uncertainties of the venture are unique in ways that are best understood by those closest to it. The challenge of managing a project's execution lies principally in addressing and resolving a series of situations but it depends also upon prescribed methods and processes. They serve the venture but they do not direct it.

When a project regime is to work in partnership with a line-of-business organisation, managing the relationship will require vigilance and sensitivity. Care is needed when contrasting patterns of working practices when the communities are required to function in concert. Different routines and assumptions can easily bring confusion, disorder, disruption and mistrust.

What is to be done by a project regime and how it is to be done in collaboration with its host organisation requires agility. A line-of-business organisation is rarely accustomed to the irregularity and adaptation commonly experienced in managing a project. In such a partnership situation, the project regime is usually found to take the lead in securing the necessary collaboration and 'acculturation' (one organisation adapting to the culture of another). In the paper 'Managing change across boundaries', engagement with existing power relations, network dependence, improvisation and 'manipulation' of the context are examined (Balogun et al., 2005). In a project regime – as in a health regime or procurement regime – the way that it is conducted becomes customary, in contrast with the habits and traditions of others.

A project regime's circumstances in responding to the unexpected can be seen as analogous to a footballer's assessment of a ball coming towards them. Its speed and direction and the player's movement relative to the pitch and the other players must determine their response. Many factors will influence the outcome. This contrasts with the experience of line-of-business processes where the analogy is more with the experience of a bowling alley. There it is the player's assessment of the position of static pins and the way in which the ball can be thrown that is the challenge. The throw is carefully pre-meditated and the player makes their throw without the direct the involvement of the other players. The context is more constant and the active dynamics that come from the interaction with other players in a football match are absent.

Local Issues Can Be the Most Stubborn

A project is not a single coherent endeavour. It is a mixture of transactions, analysis, decisions and activities that need to be continually co-ordinated and adapted. A project plan is regularly subjected to interruption from what NASA terms 'mid-course corrections'. These cause the project to realign and reset activities and intentions in response to events and rethinking as they occur. This is illustrated in the Tacking Cycle described in Figure 8.2.

Projects are exceptional both in the novelty and ambition of their agenda and in what is expected of players. In managing a project, they will sometimes be pushed beyond the limits of their own or their organisation's capacity to perform. This book considers a project as a rollercoaster of human endeavour; the conduct of the regime being a project's primary source of risk and opportunity. Systematic endeavour engages with active responses to issues that arise.

Risks can result in unexpected opportunities as well as uncertainty, hazard and constraint. They also show how the causes of project success need to be made visible and tangible before they can expect to be tamed and harnessed. Projects include the most difficult of mankind's endeavours where solutions can be difficult to find. Rittel and Webber in 'Dilemmas in a general theory of planning' refer to 'messes in which commitments have to be made based on insufficient or ambiguous information, which in turn leads to differing views on what ought to be done' (Rittel and Webber, 1973).

Many project management endeavours turn out as a triumph. In others, factors perhaps beyond the control of the project regime or the sponsor result in difficulty and even failure. In many cases, disappointments can be attributed to shortcomings in its managing or leading. In these cases the project may well have been conducted using outdated practices; ignorant of ideas and capabilities deployed in other places. The project management community needs to be more closely connected; and for many practitioners and their organisations, a more complete and coherent understanding of the discipline is required.

The remarkably wide variety of projects today and the rich mix of expertise needed to sustain them, distinguish project management from other business activity. The discipline is deployed to develop a pharmaceutical drug; refurbish an underground railway system; transform a business organisation, a software program or an IT system or to launch a spacecraft. There are profound differences in the way that projects can be and are conducted and there are great challenges in all sectors and domains.

The life-cycle presents us with a sequence of distinct stages or 'phases'; a structure that helps us to plan and assess progress and to know how and when to deploy method and other expertise. However the most challenging issues do not arise from methodology systems or technique. Most often, they stem from a project's immediate neighbourhood: the sponsors, the context; stakeholders; the project regime; political forces; commercial or cultural issues relating to risk; the use of technology; the ability of players; errors; misjudgements; misunderstandings; oversight; personal ambition misplaced; a limited capacity for social engagement between players; disputes within a project regime; a disinclination to innovate and others.

A project regime has to be capable of interpreting events unemotionally and authentically. Players should be an assembly of the most informed and professional available; but as C.L.R. James, the West Indian cricket player and writer said, 'What do they know of cricket who only cricket know?' (James, 1963). Like the able cricketer, the able project professional has to be knowledgeable about matters beyond what others might regard as the boundaries of the discipline. They need also to be a student of human behaviour, everyday philosophy and political conduct, as well as the domains from which the project is derived and to which their project is delivering.

Projects Are What We Find Them To Be

How can we become more confident and capable to manage our projects successfully and what are the root causes of success and failure? Why is it that some project management functions are so much more successful than others? One reason for this is that projects have to be progressed through events that were unforeseen or unforeseeable; requiring plan changes sometimes amounting to a critical re-direction of its affairs. Many project regimes today lack confidence or autonomy; they stumble or hesitate and show themselves to be ill-equipped to adapt. The Nine Crucial Capabilities (Table P.1), with this book, provide an agenda for review and revisions to practices in deploying their collective intention.

Managing a project through planning and control is important, but players have also to continually adapt what is to be done and how it is to be done. And while it can be difficult to manage the choice of an adaptation to change course, its implementation can be at least as problematic.

A strictly logical analysis should prove useful for tracing the sequence of actions in an engineering mechanism. It is less useful when examining an endeavour that is reliant on human and organisational behaviour. The application of logic alone works well for diagnosing problems with motorcycles, diesel locomotives and aeroplanes, but these objects function only systematically. The behaviour of people and their organisations are, however, instinctive, irrational, creative and unpredictable.

If project management was a mechanical mechanism that accepted a requirement, made a whirring noise and then produced the deliverables as specified, life would be more straightforward. When it ceased to function, we could open it up, examine the mechanism, diagnose the cause of failure and fix it. Then, as we acquired a full understanding of the logic of the mechanism and its workings, we could then readily identify all its failure modes so that new users could quickly learn how this model of machine can fail and how to fix it.

In the functioning of such a systematic sequence, choices are few. All that happens is likely to have happened before and the machine's functioning will always follow the same prescription. For a purely mechanical mechanism then, the way to achieve success, as well as to understand the modes of failure, can be readily prescribed.

Many accounts of project management practice indeed claim to rely on the supposition that all projects and project organisations function and are essentially conducted in the same way. Bodies of knowledge and other published standards promoted by project management institutions tend to be predicated in this way. This book recognises that such an approach will always have weaknesses; principally in the way that it neglects the need to respond to unexpected opportunities and constraints and the adaptation that then become required. These features make every project unique and dependent on a project regime's resolve, curiosity, inventiveness, resolution, dialogue and organisation. A project is a venture that has to be planned but it cannot be predicted; because it is subject to some discovery and subsequent adaptation.

Redirection and the Tacking Cycle

After its initial scoping and shaping, a first plan will predict a linear development of the project's progress over time. This is shown as a broken line in Figure 8.1 opposite.

Subsequent events will disturb this prediction of progress, when revisions to the requirement occur and resource constraints, fresh ideas, mistakes, errors, reworking and other interventions occur. When projects have high levels of uncertainty and complexity, events are likely to be significant and frequent.

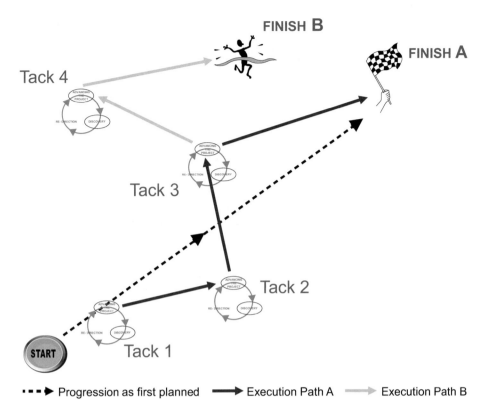

FINISH B

FINISH A

Tack 4

Tack 3

Tack 2

Tack 1

START

■ ■ ■ ▶ Progression as first planned   ──▶ Execution Path A   ──▶ Execution Path B

Figure 8.1   Discovery and Redirection
Source: 2012 © EngagementWorks Ltd.

They are shown here as Tacking Points, where a project revision results in a re-routing that takes the project down a new path, on which the project is then to progress.

In this representation of a project's progression, the path from Tack 1 to Tack 2 the project is diverted by a misunderstanding. The path to Tack 3 is then taken in response to a competitor's re-positioning in the market and when it is decided that an additional product is to be added. These are delivered At 'Finish A' and 'Finish B'. At Tack 4, selected features of the second product are discontinued to bring the product to market earlier than was originally intended.

In undertaking projects having high levels of uncertainty and complexity, a project regime must regularly address and resolve these Tacking Points by following the Tacking Cycle.

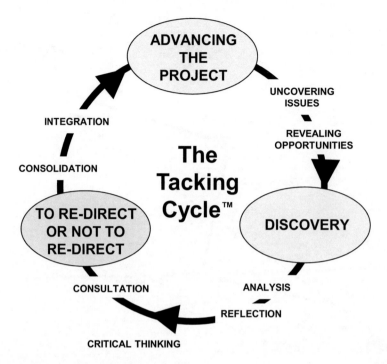

Figure 8.2   The Tacking Cycle
Source: 2012 © EngagementWorks Ltd.

According to Helmuth Karl Bernhard von Moltke, 'No battle plan survives contact with the enemy and War is a matter of expedients'. The same principle applies when managing a project and the Tacking Cycle carries us through the adaptation that may be needed to determine and validate a true course.

The cycle to be followed is shown in Figure 8.2. As any project *Advances* constraints, insights, barriers, objections, inappropriate planning assumptions, risks (up-side and down-side) and other factors emerge and become apparent for the first time. These *Discoveries* need to be properly understood and their significance shared and evaluated. If it is judged necessary to act upon what has been discovered by following a new path, *Redirection* will change either the goals to be achieved and/or the means of achieving them.

In practice the amount of time and effort devoted to exercising this cycle is often far greater than is realised. To exploit the potential of the Tacking Cycle, a project regime's key players as a group, need to be able to explore the issues fully, decide on a course of action together and then make it happen. For this, they will need a robust Engagement Capability (see Chapter 4).

A Regime's Adaptation Goals

Adaptation is a regular feature of managing a project. This pattern has to be regarded as normal, often to the chagrin of players. While a project regime cannot anticipate the events that call for Tacking, it needs to be ready to give a good account of itself when the need for re-planning occurs. The Tacking Cycle offers a guide to project players in the form of a logical scrutiny; to decide whether a mid-course correction is appropriate and if so, what the new direction should be.

A project regime's readiness to adapt also depends on its readiness to reach a set of adaptation goals – in the same way that a regime's capacity for social engagement depends on its capacity to realise its Engagement Goals (see Chapter 4). Adaptation Goals are shown in Figure 8.3 below, and these are developed further in the following pages.

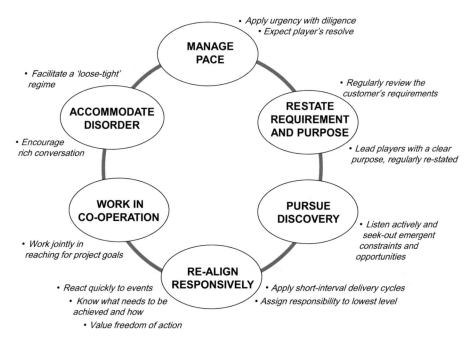

Figure 8.3   A Regime's Adaptation Goals

Source: 2012 © EngagementWorks Ltd.

MANAGE PACE

Maximising the pace of progress requires effective and efficient adaptation in response to events. Effective, in that cases for adaptation are well judged; efficient in that the methods used to advance the project are fit-for-purpose and implemented without delay. Early warning of an up-coming course correction should help players to comprehend the issues, expedite the adaptation and moderate the accompanying risks. A regime's 'connections' (Chapter 4) will help to refine the choices available for the new plan and to enrich it.

RESTATE REQUIREMENT AND PURPOSE

A project's requirements and purpose often change and a regime needs to keep its players up-to-date with progress and issues. Sensitivity to opinion, concerns and promptings are important, as is the need for regime leaders to share information relating to current events. One-to-one visual management and personal presentations are often the most effective and appreciated means of broadcasting and enabling player's insightful questioning.

PURSUE DISCOVERY

Players need at all times to listen and reflect; remembering actions and events and continually posing questions, as led by their curiosity and persistent scrutiny. This should enhance their understanding of issues and the likely consequences of imagined scenarios. Leaders need to be intent on gathering intelligence and opinion from other players.

REALIGN RESPONSIVELY

The dialogue between leaders and their planning should be witnessed by other stakeholders; applying short-interval delivery cycles. Delay, whatever the cause, should be remedied assertively and responsibilities assigned to the lowest level possible. Autonomy and freedom of action, properly managed, should moderate procrastination and devolve professional experience in the regime.

WORK IN CO-OPERATION

Engagement and collaboration depend on resolve and candour. Every opportunity for players to be co-located/meet regularly/jointly problem-solve should be used. Leadership should be expected from every player: project management is a play of leadership. Negotiations should be conducted from positions of wide-ranging knowledge and clear purpose.

ACCOMMODATE DISORDER

Responsibilities need to be assuredly assigned and supported; relying on connected autonomy. Strive to build trust. Apparent disorder can sometimes obscure that focused and committed effort is being conducted. Leadership should be encouraged to moderate behaviour in the organisation, using the principle of 'loose-tight' (see Chapter 9).

The Myth of Automated Collaboration

A proliferation of software tools and techniques is now claimed to sustain project management performance and reliability. They are systems that collect, collate and filter, record project data and distribute it, track progress and prompt actions that have been planned.

Numerous software tool suppliers promote 'collaboration software'. But this is can be regarded as a contradiction of terms. To collaborate depends on resolve, dialogue and organisation, sensing, questioning, deciding and showing the way. The efficiency of these activities will in some ways depend on IT systems, but collaboration is essentially achieved through the project players' behaviour and collective conduct. Information technology is an important resource to achieve efficiency, but it is not a primary requirement for decision-making. A recent advertisement reads as follows (the name 'Acme' has been used in place of the brand name):

> By providing a 360-degree view of all workplace activities, Acme helps both team members and management alike to better understand and organise their work. As work is completed, team members can log time, provide updates, keep work progressing or complete tasks – ensuring your projects and top objectives get done. Acme empowers workers to contribute maximum value and gives executives visibility into all projects and other work, creating workplace harmony by enfranchising workers and informing executives.

The implication here is that to manage 'all workplace activities' of a project requires only that information is effectively initiated, managed and shared.

But what of problem-solving; the learning from the project experience and emergent issues; the need for dialogue and to persuade, promote and work out how to incorporate new ideas and overcome difficulties? Surely these matters are germane to *'creating workplace harmony by enfranchising workers and informing executives'*. Acme cannot be offering the services that they claim, much beyond information processing and exchange. Acme themselves seem to be locked into the trap of the 'paradigm paradox', seeing project management as a set of prescribable working processes.

Here, Acme are offering an information technology (IT) solution to resolve an issue (collaboration) that requires the attention of project players who must share a variety of perspectives, knowledge, skills, opinion, interests and choices. These are factors that must be digested and in some way reconciled for a project to progress. Collaboration depends upon close rapport, engagement, negotiation, political sensitivity and resolve.

This story of 'Acme' might serve to illustrate to the reader how project management needs to be recognised as a social endeavour. In seeking a strong pace of progress and reliability, the emphasis of the work needs to focus on the human and organisational behaviour.

Professional Pointers

• We cannot know with certainty of the outcome or consequences of decisions made today.

• A project is an expedition that has few prescriptions on which to rely.

• Projects are expeditions that evolve successfully through their adaptation.

• Methodology and techniques serve project management; they do not direct it.

• A project regime working in partnership with a 'business as usual' organisation requires care.

• Many of a project's challenges arise from local difficulties rather than from customer or user.

• 'What do they know of cricket who only cricket know?'

- A plan is rarely a safe prediction of what will happen.

- Collaboration can be aided by information systems but it cannot be conducted by this way.

- Adaptation can be planned but nevertheless entirely depends on human skill and ingenuity.

References

Balogun, J. et al. (2005). Managing change across boundaries: Boundary-shaking practices. *British Journal of Management*, 6(4): 261–78.

Hansen, M.T. (2009). *Collaboration: How Leaders Avoid the Traps, Create Unity, and Reap Big Results*. Cambridge, MA: Harvard Business Press.

James, C.L.R. (1963). *Beyond a Boundary*. London: Stanley Paul.

Rittel, H.W.J. and Webber, M.M. (1973). Dilemmas in a general theory of planning. *Policy Sciences*, 4(2): 155–69.

Chapter 9

The Project's Maturity

Ensuring Project Reliability and Sustaining Continuous Improvement

> Performing tenaciously and successfully as a 'seasoned' dynamic community that sustains its capacity to improve.
>
> *Refer to the Nine Crucial Capabilities*

Introduction

When we think of the maturity of project management conduct and practices, we are considering the advantages of working arrangements and their successive improvements that raise the usefulness and value of a project's outcomes, deliverables and products.

Many project management practitioners have heard of project management maturity (PMM) or 'maturity models', though perhaps some are not aware of their origins. The principles are derived from Quality Management. Total Quality Management (TQM) is a management approach first adopted by businesses in the 1980s and 1990s to manage the optimisation of product processes and quality.

The TQM model led the Software Engineering Institute at Carnegie Mellon University to develop the Capability Maturity Model (CMM) that in turn provided the foundations for most project management maturity models today.

These ideas for raising the maturity of process performance were originally developed to improve the efficiency and effectiveness of a regularly repeated end-to-end process as found in manufacturing. The purpose there is the optimisation of a process to improve the quality of products, minimise waste, lower inventory levels and reduce costs. The purpose of raising the maturity of a project regime is different. As it is understood when viewed through the ideas expressed in this book, a project regime's maturity is its capacity to maximise the project's pace of progress (see Chapter 6). This depends, amongst other factors, on its ability to deliver and to respond to unforeseen events.

The established models of project management maturity are largely concerned with processes and practices. They include OPM3 (PMI), PMM (APM) and P3M3 and P2MM (Axelos), and use concepts from CMM. PMI's OPM3, perhaps the most widely known project management maturity model, offers a vast disaggregation and complex mapping of 'organisational maturity', prescribing 600 'best practices', 3,000 'capabilities' and over 4,000 relationships between capabilities. It gives little attention to the behaviours of the project players and their organisation on which organisational performance depends. The behaviours in question here include thinking, social engagement, collaboration, dialogue and persistence.

A project regime's principal challenge lies in its ability to respond and adapt to circumstances that were not planned for: events that will then require organisational changes and re-planning for the project to progress. Here, agility, prompt responses and adaptation are required; addressing the question, 'How is a project regime able to maximise its pace of progress while also discovering and accommodating opportunities and constraints and managing its redirection?' (see Figure 8.1 and the Tacking Cycle).

Regime Maturity Goals

Managing a project's pace of progress relies on the players and their regime's ability to adapt. The Nine Crucial Capabilities (see Table P.1) all of which are examined in this book, have a critical part to play in securing and advancing project management maturity.

Figure 5.1 presents two 'Aspects' of project management. One addresses the necessities for procedure or 'Essential Schemas' and is labelled Methodological and Operational Capabilities (MOCs), the other the necessity for organisational agility or 'Vital Behaviours' – labelled Human and Organisational Capabilities

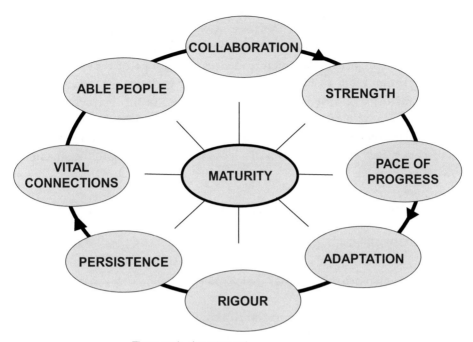

These goals also represent
- The Nine Crucial Capabilities of a project regime
- The Single Minded project regime chapter headings

Figure 9.1   Project Regime Maturity

Source: 2012 © EngagementWorks Ltd.

(HOCs). The former are comprehensively provided for in professional credentialling, certification and in PM maturity models. Project Regime Maturity offers a more comprehensive solution for an organisation seeking to manage projects more ably and reliably.

As presented in Figure 9.1, emphasis is placed on HOCs. Crucial Capability five, 'Rigour', captures the MOCs. 'Maturity', the ninth Crucial Capability, relies on the remaining seven.

FACTORS CONTRIBUTING TO REGIME MATURITY

Unlike the human condition, the passage of time does not of itself bring maturity to a project regime. Instead it is the players' pursuit of improvement, learning, rigour, professionalism and enterprise that expedite its emergence from adolescence.

Terry Cooke-Davies and Andrew Arzymanow, in their paper 'The maturity of project management in different industries' (2002), examine the variability in project management practices in a range of industries. Their study confirms there to be significant conduct variations to practices and that the maturity of a regime is a primary success factor. Petrochemicals is cited as an example of an industry that has matured more than most and it is suggested that this may well be related to cost reduction programmes in oil discovery and extraction industries deployed in response to the sustained low oil price in the 1980s.

Other factors that stimulate greater Regime Maturity include:

- A leadership that is resolved to excel.

- Diligence of dialogue (see Chapter 4).

- Effective organisation and working arrangements.

- Single-mindedness.

- Compliance and deployment of methodology and standards.

- The level of personal experience and the development of players.

- Strengthening of regime autonomy.

- The accommodation of stakeholders' preferences.

- Market pressure for improving performance and reliability.

- A culture that accepts adaptation and agility.

- Ambition to improve the pace of progress.

- Attention to human and organisational behaviour.

- Collaboration/partnership/alliancing with stakeholders.

- Deploying the players' legacy of professional experience.

The patterns of progression of major projects is rarely predictable. They are voyages of discovery, progressing through regular planning and from the clues and cues that emerge as they proceed.

A project will be regarded differently depending on people's perspective and interests: e.g. something necessary to bring about change; something that has a life-cycle; a social endeavour; delivering a strategic necessity; something to subdue as an opponent or enemy; something that is relied upon by a business to secure its future; a means of job creation; a venture that has not been attempted before; a necessary evil; an enterprise that promises salvation etc. This way at looking at an organisation as a system is developed by Peter Checkland in Soft Systems Methodology (SSM) (Checkland and Scholes, 1990).

Sustaining and Disruptive Innovation

Like any professional discipline, project management has learned to apply the benefits of continual (or 'sustaining') innovation to enable improved understanding and practices. Examples of continual innovation include earned value, risk management, information systems, risk attitude and critical chain. Less attention has in the past been devoted to human and organisational behaviour as a subject for new thinking and innovation.

Aside from continual innovation, the following describes the phenomenon of 'disruptive innovation'; a mechanism to bring about an advance in capability. It is an abrupt occurrence: that can happen in any branch of human endeavour. Examples have included the use of a chronometer in navigation, sufficiently accurate to determine longitude (John Harrison) and in science the application of the quantum in the understanding of physics (Max Planck).

Disruptive and Sustaining Innovation

Disruptive innovation is a term first used by Professor Clayton Christensen of Harvard Business School (Christensen, 1997). He describes disruptive innovation in marketing terms as creating a new market and value network and eventually proceeding to disrupt an existing market and value network to displace an earlier technology.

Examples of disruptive innovation from history include the low-cost motor vehicle (Ford); continuous improvement (Kaizen); the mobile phone (Motorola); the microprocessor (Intel); penicillin (Alexander Fleming); the iPod (Apple Inc.); the Jacquard loom (Joseph Marie Jacquard) and the limited liability company (fifteenth-century English law).

In contrast and by way of example, the more recent development of the mobile phone incorporating camera, computer, internet connection and display is the product of sustaining innovation. These are innovations that bring improvement to the value and utility of an existing product, whereas disruptive innovation 'breaks the mould' – initiating a radically new creation that displaces predecessors.

It may be that the discipline of project management could at some time reach a tipping point to then transform as a result of some disruptive innovation. Many see project management as a discipline to be running short of the sustaining innovations needed to bring about the transformation that is needed. Certainly, stronger and more reliable performance is available to a project when its players are fully engaged to exploit the opportunities offered by human and organisational as well as logical and systematic endeavour. An attempt is made in this book to build the case for this possibility as it is now conducted by a minority of project regimes.

Diversity and Decision-Making

Working arrangements between stakeholders, suppliers and other parties are becoming closer as project organisations and their activities become increasingly interdependent. There is growing pressure to increase the pace of progress of projects; for instance adopting agile practices that rely on short-interval delivery cycles and devolved responsibilities. These can be witnessed in the accounts of the Andrew Field project (see Chapter 1) and the Rocky Flats project described later in this chapter.

Expectations of project delivery are continually rising, bringing changes to traditional forms of organisation. By way of example, on London Heathrow Airport's Terminal 5 programme, contractors working on some of the projects were required as a condition of their deal, to serve as members of the core project regime, managing multi-supplier construction projects.

A project organisation is sustained in a continual state of transition, with the range of tasks, their interdependence and their status regularly adapting and changing. Decisions for planning, prioritising, assessing, deploying resources, resolving issues, engaging with stakeholders, collaborating and responding to events, all rely strongly on patterns of social engagement and connection between players, functions and other interests.

The products of project management can be seen as the result of choices and decisions made by and within the project regime. They determine a project's pace of progress and the routes to be followed. Groups within a regime form and disband in innumerable ways, pursuing goals and exploring issues. Social as well as commercial pressures on organisations encourage the devolution of responsibilities and this has led to changes to the character and patterns of decision-making.

In responding to pressures to perform and compete, there is in many quarters an abiding appetite for discovery. A diversity of perspectives and abilities in an organisation, when properly exploited, can bring a richness of resolve, dialogue and enterprise – as demonstrated by Scott E. Page in *The Difference* (Page, 2007). Initiatives to enlarge player constituencies where issues, options and opinions can be more widely explored, are a response to civic or commercial goals for strengthening competitive advantage.

An interesting trend now emerging is to extend a project's resources into 'crowdsourcing' (Rouse, 2011). According to the Merriam-Webster Dictionary this is the practice of obtaining services, ideas or content by soliciting contributions from a large group of people, especially from an online community, as well as from traditional employees or suppliers. However, the capacity of a regime to extend the range of its dialogue community often proves problematic. It could be that adding connections to a wider field of interest is inhibited by a legacy of hierarchical behaviours and the paradigm paradox (see Chapter 4).

An Occupation Elevating to a Profession

We have reached a point in the development of project management following the formalisation of the discipline through the 1960s and 1980s, where a new understanding needs to be devised, consolidated and adopted. Project professionals now find it increasingly apparent that there is more to managing a project than is characterised by a linear and predictable sequence of life-cycle standards, processes and methodology. Unfortunately these aspects, while crucial to conducting project management, have in recent years somehow distracted practitioners away from the development of practices that address human and organisational conduct.

A price is now being paid for this. Human and organisational behaviour is the arena in which project work is planned and organised, where project issues are argued and resolved and where the decisions are made. A project regime can find itself challenged by a technical problem, a programme realignment, the shortcomings of a sub-contractor or the resignation of a key player; but for it to prosper in the face of difficulties, there has to be a common resolve among stakeholders, social engagement, the richness and rigour of dialogue and a functioning organisation.

Many of the project management challenges that continue to defeat or elude some project regimes are readily accommodated as part of the familiar working practices of others. Innovation comes from insight, competence, dialogue and argument and through connections with other professionals in their industry and beyond it. Without it necessarily being intended, strong and powerful methods lay beyond the reach of many project management communities. An important occupation continues with a disparity of practices that prevent it from attaining the standing that is attainable and is urgently sought.

To enable a more effective exchange and consolidation of good practice, project management professionals and other players need to share a common understanding of all that is involved in managing a project and the challenges that it can present. Such a comprehensive picture is not yet available. As in any discipline, it is important to view and to scrutinise the whole picture, otherwise people's comprehension will be disparate and distorted; placing important matters beyond false boundaries and out of the reach of their adherents and advocates.

An academy in which human and organisational behaviour can be studied and practised could substantially raise the abilities of professionals to manage projects. The curriculum would be delivered most effectively through experiential methods of learning and development.

A more complete grasp of the nature of project management is needed to relieve players who find themselves having to 'feel their way' forward. Players need to lift clear of what the late Donald Schön referred to as the 'swampy lowlands', where there are few guiding principles, frameworks or models to guide them through the labyrinth (Schön, 1983). We can sense that the 'boring and repetitive' factors referred to by Martin Barnes and Peter Gershon (see Introduction) relate to these issues, many of which are regarded as indefinable. They are conundrums that need to be unpicked, placed more centrally in our consciousness and 'broken in'. For early man, the potential value of wild horses, while clearly apparent, remained dormant until communities learned to 'break them in'. We now have to approach these 'boring and repetitive failures' with some passion and appreciative enquiry: to harness solutions to what for many are long-standing barriers to progress.

Aspiring to Professional Status

The discipline is caught in a catch-22. Project practitioners struggle to be recognised as responsible for project decisions and their outcomes because it is said that they are not recognised as professionals. And they are not recognised as professionals because it is said that they are not expected to exercise full professional responsibility. But such an enigmatic proposition should be unacceptable to those worthy of advocating professional status. There has to be a root cause to explain the hesitation now being shown in the pursuit of professional recognition.

In considering this question, the authors of *Professionalization of Project Management*, a PMI publication, make the following observation:

> *Project management leaders recognise that they do not have as firm a grasp of many of the professional characteristics necessary to attain professional status. Yet, the same leadership does not recognise as many challenges as do other occupations (Zwerman et al., 2004: 154).*

The message here aligns with the claim above that the discipline has been unable and even unwilling to acquire an understanding of the 'whole picture' or what is termed here as 'complete project management'. It is as though there is a shortage of professional ambition. Securing a complete understanding must surely be a prerequisite for any campaign likely to secure professional standing and public recognition. As a first step, such a thesis has to be established by a representative body and then communicated and promoted in way that can be understood by the wider professional community.

A fresh perspective is offered here, recognising the crucial importance of the behaviours of players and groups of players. It seeks to show the advantages of a more open agile and responsive form of organisation while sustaining the rigour of a disciplined approach, principles and practices. Project management as a discipline must become more robust in its handling of ambiguity, complexity, uncertainty and setback than many regimes are now able to achieve. Only when the importance of these critical factors becomes well-articulated can we expect to decide on the aspects of behaviour, individually and in groups, that need our greatest attention.

This book also seeks to show that a regime serving a line-of-business enterprise will always depend on its host being perceptive and informed: able to champion their commission as well as to harness it. Without robust sponsorship, a project regime will most likely turn in mediocre performance. Growing a competent and dynamic regime and culture must, for a sponsor, demand high priority: encouraging players to be resolved and actively engaged, collaborating and adapting to circumstances as they evolve.

Some in the project management community now claim that the discipline has attained a professional status. For this to be true, the role of the project management practitioner needs to be seen to stand alone and be separately and wholly accountable for delivery. This is a situation in which few practitioners find themselves.

The Value Zone of an Enterprise

The 'Value Zone' in an organisation is the place where the greatest value to the customer is given and from where delivery is assured. For an increasing number of organisations, the project regime is or is becoming the Value Zone of their enterprise.

In Vineet Nayar's book *Employees First, Customers Second* (Nayar, 2010), he explains his experience in taking on the role of CEO of HCL Technologies, a $6 billion leading global technology and IT company based in India. He recounts how shortly after his appointment, visiting a very satisfied HCL customer of their 'Transformational Outsourcing' services and seeing the customer's delight. He saw then for the first time how the work of HCL's salespeople, systems architects and implementation teams had together become The Value Zone of his business – a business that hitherto had gained a strong reputation for competitive advantage primarily from its technical prowess. The R&D function, while remaining important to HCL had been displaced through the evolution of the outsourcing industry. Maturity had been redefined and the business's earlier pre-eminence in technology innovation had been the key to success – but the world had changed.

A Triumph of Collaboration: Rocky Flats

Let's first take a look at an example of a project contractor who in their business plan and project strategy deliberately chose to break away from traditional practices concerning project management, organisational roles and hierarchy. Rocky Flats was a major project in US waste disposal in which senior managers decided to adopt alternative organisational practices as a way to transform their venture, placing a new emphasis on the players' collaboration.

In 1989, Kaiser-Hill Inc. was awarded a contract to 'clean up' the nuclear weapons facility at Rocky Flats in Colorado, USA (PMI, 2007). For 37 years Rocky Flats had been a top-secret facility manufacturing nuclear weapons. Following its closure, the site contained contaminated soil and groundwater that had been left behind. These materials included half a million cubic metres of material containing radioactive plutonium waste.

As an indication of the uncertainties regarding cost and duration of the clean-up prior to the contract being awarded, estimates had ranged from $37 billion over 60 years to $17 billion over 15 years. When the contract was awarded to Kaiser-Hill, for $6 billion over six years, Howard Gilpin, a vice president who led preparation of the successful proposal, was quoted to have said: 'our proposal depended largely on techniques and processes that no one then had even thought of'. Kaiser-Hill was awarded the project together with some significant commercial risks. Their enterprise would have to resolve some seriously challenging issues, many of which they knew had yet to be discovered. The risk of failure was high, but so were the rewards that they saw and their resolve to be successful. Kaiser-Hill reckoned that they had the necessary ingenuity and enterprise to resolve the problems.

On his first arrival at the site, the project manager was physically threatened by the plant's personnel then resisting its closure. He made monthly presentations to the workforce and to locally elected officials; gradually winning over support for arrangements that would include the deployment of these same local staff to undertake the clean-up. The choice was made not to appoint externally sourced specialist labour, an arrangement that would have been routine for this kind of operation. It was recognised that the people already in place knew the plant well and could be turned to become supporters. They were in fact to make a major contribution to the success of the project: helping to devise and implement many of the novel techniques and processes that were developed.

The project regime worked in partnership with the Department of Defense and the US Energy Department and developed radically innovative packaging systems for the storage and transportation of contaminated equipment and waste. The project manager reported that nothing was left to chance: 'That need to manage every piece of the project was a significant challenge'. Considerable ingenuity was deployed at all levels of the project organisation. The work was completed 14 months ahead of schedule, coming in at more than $500 million under budget; and the project was awarded the Project Management Institute's 'Project of the Year' in 2006. Rocky Flats, the site of the original weapons plant, is now classed as a National Wildlife Refuge.

It had been a complex project full of uncertainties and risk. The achievement was the result of a culture of controlled risk, discovery and incentive. Evidently there was solid professionalism, determination, imagination, engagement and collaboration between groups of players from within and outside the Kaiser-Hill organisation. It was also characterised by a rigorous methodology and tight project management disciples. Kaiser-Hill implemented a process of scenario planning, scoping, cost and schedule variance analysis to identify deviations at an early stage, while concurrently implementing an active and closely orchestrated policy of devolving responsibility to every reporting level. An open and business-like partnership with the people employed also characterised the style of supervision and the relationships with sub-contractors and government regulators.

The working arrangements deployed on the Kaiser-Hill project regime at Rocky Flats benefited from the regime's capacity to adapt. Success was also assured both by a robust understanding of the requirement and a thorough understanding of nuclear technology. And as the project evolved, through the player's on-going learning, confidence grew – enabling the development of practical planning and control.

The regime benefited from embracing Complete Project Management (see Chapter 5). A rigorous methodology was applied; but at the same time there was authentic social engagement and collaboration between the players that included government regulators, sub-contractors and local authorities. This thorough project management enterprise was also key to the project's pace of progress (see Chapter 4) and resulted in a very considerable reduction, not only to the original cost estimates but also to its duration. Profitability was strong.

Professional Pointers

• When viewed through the lens of this book, project management maturity serves to enhance a project's pace of progress.

• When viewed through the ideas expressed in this book, project management maturity is the capacity that it has to maximise its pace of progress unlike the human condition, the passage of time does not necessarily bring maturity.

• The maturity of a project regime is a primary success factor for the projects that it manages.

• The progress of major projects is rarely predictable. They are voyages of discovery.

• Disruptive innovation creates a new market and value network and eventually goes on to disrupt an existing market and value network to displace an earlier technology.

• Many see this discipline to be running short of the sustaining innovations needed to bring the transformation that is needed.

• A diversity of perspectives and abilities in an organisation, when properly exploited, can bring a richness of resolve, dialogue and enterprise.

• There has to be a root cause that explains the hesitation now experienced in the pursuit of professional recognition.

• For an increasing number of organisations, the project regime is or is becoming the Value Zone of their enterprise.

References

Checkland, P. and Scholes, J. (1990). *Soft Systems Methodology in Action*. New York: Wiley.

Christensen, C. (1997). *The Innovator's Dilemma: When New Technologies Cause Great Firms to Fail*. Boston, MA: Harvard Business School Press.

Cooke-Davies, T. and Arzymanow, A. (2002). The maturity of project management in different industries: An investigation into variations between project management models. *International Journal of Project Management*, 21(6): 471–8.

Nayar, V. (2010). *Employees First, Customers Second*. Boston, MA: Harvard Business School Press.

Page, S.E. (2007). *The Difference: How the Power of Diversity Creates Better Groups, Firms, Schools, and Societies*. Princeton, NJ: Princeton University Press.

PMI [Hunsberger, K.] (2007). Finding closure. *PM Network*, January, 31–6. Available at: http://www.pmi.org/About-Us/Our-Professional-Awards/~/media/PDF/Awards/PMN0107_Rockyflats.ashx [accessed 7 May 2014].

Rouse, M. (2011). *Crowdsourcing*. Retrieved from SearchCIO. Available at: http://searchcio.techtarget.com/definition/crowdsourcing [accessed 11 May 2013].

Schön, D. (1983). *The Reflective Practitioner: How Professionals Think in Action*. New York: Basic Books.

Zwerman, B.L., Thomas, J.L. and Haydt, S. (2004). *Professionalization of Project Management: Exploring the Past to Map the Future*. Newtown Square, PA: PMI.

Index